# COOKBOOK

# KETO DIET

## COOKBOOK FOR BEGINNER

*Hope Preston*

# Table of Contents

# INTRODUCTION

# Welcome to Your Keto Journey

## Personal note or story about the keto journey

### The Start of a New Chapter

I faced challenges with my weight, energy levels, and overall well-being for years. Like others, I had experimented with diets and workout routines without much success. I felt trapped in a cycle of fluctuating weight. My confidence was at an all-time low.

### Uncovering the Magic of Keto

One day, I came across the concept of the ketogenic diet. The notion of following a low-carb eating plan piqued my interest, though I was initially skeptical. How could consuming fat possibly lead to weight loss? However, as I delved deeper into research and encountered success stories, I became increasingly convinced to give it a shot. The science behind achieving ketosis seemed logical.

### The Beginning

I had to bid farewell to my carbs and embrace fats instead. The initial weeks posed challenges as my body adjusted to this approach. I faced the keto flu" symptoms, including fatigue and irritability. I was determined to persevere.

### Reaping the Rewards

With time, I began noticing transformations. My energy levels surged, bidding farewell to the midday slumps that had plagued me for years. My mental clarity improved, enhancing my focus on tasks. Notably, I started shedding weight healthily. Controlling cravings became easier. My relationship with food underwent positive changes.

### A Fresh Lifestyle

What initially began as a diet soon became a lifestyle choice for me. I developed a passion for preparing keto meals and experimenting with recipes in the kitchen. Crafting dishes that nourished my body while pleasing my palate brought me joy.

### Navigating Obstacles and Celebrating Victories

Undoubtedly, the journey had its share of ups and downs.
There were moments when I made mistakes or felt disheartened. The support from the keto community, both online and offline, was truly invaluable. Knowing that others were going through the journey made an impact.

### Expressing My Enthusiasm

My success with the keto diet motivated me to share my story and knowledge with others. This cookbook reflects my love for the ketogenic lifestyle and my desire to assist others in reaching their health aspirations. Each recipe in this book has been thoughtfully created to be tasty, nourishing, and simple to prepare.

### Closing Remarks

The diet has transformed my life in ways I never imagined possible. It has restored my health, boosted my confidence, and revitalized me in ways I never thought achievable. I am eager for you to experience these advantages firsthand. Remember, every journey begins with a step, and by picking up this book, you have already taken that step.

# The Basics of the Keto Diet: Key Principles, Health Benefits, and Cultural Background

The Keto Diet, also known as the ketogenic diet, emphasizes consuming amounts of fat and low levels of carbohydrates. It has gained popularity because of its health benefits in weight management and overall metabolic health. Initially used in the 20th century, the Keto Diet has become a mainstream option for individuals looking to improve their well-being. This article delves into the aspects of the Keto Diet, its advantages for health, and practical suggestions for integrating it into routines.

## Introduction to the Keto Diet

The Keto Diet revolves around significantly reducing carbohydrate intake while increasing consumption. This change in balance induces a metabolic state known as ketosis, where fats are utilized as the energy source instead of glucose. The fundamental elements of the Keto Diet consist of:

- Fat: 70 75% of daily caloric intake should be derived from fats like avocados, nuts, seeds, and oils.
- Moderate Protein: Aim for 20 25% of calories from protein sources such as meat, fish, and eggs.
- Low Carbohydrates: Limit carbohydrate intake to around 5 10% of calories by focusing on starchy vegetables and select fruits.

## The Keto Diets Health Benefits

### Managing Weight

One of the advantages of the Keto Diet is its effectiveness in weight management. By cutting down on carbs, the body uses up its glycogen reserves. It starts burning fat for fuel. This results in a decrease in body fat and aids in achieving and maintaining weight.

### Boosted Energy Levels

Being in ketosis provides an energy supply from fat stores, leading to stable energy levels throughout the day. Many individuals following the Keto Diet mention feeling less hungry and experiencing energy dips compared to a carb diet.

### Sharper Mental Focus

The brain efficiently utilizes ketones as an energy source, which can improve function and mental clarity. This is why many people on the Keto Diet notice focus and concentration.

### Blood Sugar Management

By restricting intake, the keto diet can assist in regulating blood sugar levels, making it beneficial for those with insulin resistance or type 2 diabetes. Additionally, this diet may reduce the reliance on insulin and other diabetes medications.

Longevity and Well-being

Some studies indicate that following the Keto Diet could potentially promote life by reducing inflammation, enhancing heart health, and supporting aging. However, further research is required to grasp these long-term advantages.

# Integrating the Keto Diet into Everyday Life

**Simple Substitutions and Suggestions**

Transitioning to the Keto Diet can be made more accessible with substitutions and suggestions:

- Swap out bread and pasta for low-carb alternatives like cauliflower rice and zucchini noodles.
- Opt for fats such as olive, coconut, and butter when cooking.
- Choose nuts, seeds, cheese, and avocados as chips and cookies snacks.

**Meal Preparation**

Planning your meals ahead of time can facilitate adherence to the Keto Diet. Concentrate on crafting meals that are rich in fat but low in carbs, like:

- Breakfast: Scrambled eggs paired with spinach and avocado.
- Lunch: Grilled chicken salad drizzled with olive oil dressing.
- Dinner: Steak served with vegetables.
- Snacks: Sunflower seeds, cheese slices, or boiled eggs.

Smart Grocery Shopping for Keto. When you're putting together your grocery list, it's crucial to include the right items for a successful Keto diet. Make sure to add veggies like leafy greens, broccoli, and cauliflower; protein sources such as meat, fish, and eggs; healthy fats like avocados, nuts, and oils; and dairy products like full-fat cheese, cream, and yogurt. This way, you're always prepared with the right ingredients for your Keto meals.

Cooking your meals at home gives you control over what goes into your food. It helps you stick to your Keto plan. Try baking, grilling, or sautéing for fat, low-carb dishes. Don't hesitate to experiment with herbs and spices for added flavor without the carbs.

Living the Keto Lifestyle: It's More Than Just Food. Incorporating physical activities like walking, jogging, or strength training into your daily routine is a crucial part of the Keto lifestyle. It's about what you eat and how you approach life. Sharing meals with loved ones can make dining more enjoyable and provide social support. By embracing this holistic approach, you're not just following a diet, but a lifestyle that promotes overall well-being.

Prioritizing your health is key to embracing the spirit of the Keto lifestyle. By following these practices and staying physically active, you can lead a more satisfying life.

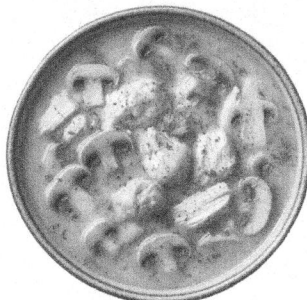

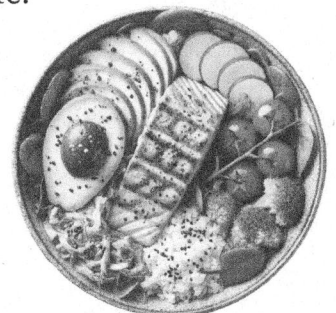

# Chapter 1:
# Navigating the Keto Diet:
# Foods to Eat and Avoid

The keto diet, short for the ketogenic diet, is a way of eating that focuses on carbs and high fats to trigger ketosis in the body. During ketosis, the body uses fat for the energy of carbs, leading to benefits like weight loss, increased energy, and better mental focus. This article provides tips and insights on what foods to include and avoid while following the keto diet.

## Foods to Eat on the Keto Diet

### Proteins

Recommended Options: Beef, pork, lamb, chicken, turkey, fish ( varieties like salmon and mackerel) and seafood.

Why They're Choices: These protein sources contain amino acids and healthy fats that help maintain muscle mass and overall well-being. Fatty fish are particularly beneficial due to their omega-3 acids, which support heart health and reduce inflammation.

Tips for Choosing and Cooking:

- Opt for grass-fed or meats when available.
- Choose caught fish rather than farmed options.
- Cook proteins by grilling, baking, or sautéing in fats such as olive oil or butter.

### Vegetables

Top Picks: greens like spinach, kale, and Swiss chard; cruciferous veggies like broccoli, cauliflower, and Brussels sprouts; and other carb options like zucchini, bell peppers, cucumbers, and asparagus.

Reasons to Choose Them: These veggies are choices because they're low in carbs but packed with fiber, vitamins, and minerals. They support gut health, offer nutrients, and help you feel full.

Tips for Choosing and Cooking:

- Go for frozen veggies without any sauces or sugars.
- Try roasting, steaming, or sautéing the vegetables with fats to bring out their flavors and make the nutrients more accessible.
- Get creative by using vegetables as swaps for foods (e.g., cauliflower rice or zucchini noodles).

### Healthy. Oils

Best Choices: olive oil, avocado oil, coconut oil, butter, ghee, avocados, nuts (almonds, walnuts, macadamia nuts), and seeds (chia seeds, flaxseeds).

Why They're Recommended: Healthy fats play a role in the keto diet by providing lasting energy and supporting ketosis. They also help with cell structure, hormone production, and nutrient absorption.

Tips for Choosing and Preparing:

- Opt for olive oil for salads and light cooking.
- Use coconut oil. Avocado oil for cooking at temperatures.
- Include a variety of nuts and seeds in your meals as snacks or toppings for salads and yogurt.

### Dairy Products

Top Picks: cheese (cheddar, mozzarella, goat cheese), heavy cream, sour cream, and Greek yogurt (unsweetened total fat).

Why They're Recommended: fat dairy options offer fats and proteins that help keep you full and maintain a balanced diet. They are ingredients for keto recipes.

Tips for Choosing and Preparing:

- Pick unsweetened dairy items to avoid added sugars and extra carbs.
- Enjoy cheese as a snack. Incorporate it into dishes like casseroles or salads.
- Use cream and sour cream in sauces or desserts.

## Foods You Should Steer Clear of While Following the Keto Diet

### High Carb Options

Types of Food to Avoid: Bread, noodles, rice, cereal, and various grains.

Reasons for Avoiding Them: These items are packed with carbs, which can cause spikes in blood sugar levels and knock you out of ketosis. They don't offer much nutrition when following a keto eating plan.

### Strategies for Handling Challenges:

- Opt for alternatives such as cauliflower rice, zucchini noodles, and baked goods made with almond flour.
- Plan your meals to resist the urge to indulge in food.

### Sweet Treats

Types of Food to Stay Away From: Sweets like candy bars, pastries, ice cream, and sugary beverages (sodas and fruit juices).

Reasons for Steering Clear: Sweet snacks can cause blood sugar spikes. Provide empty calories that may hinder your keto journey.

### Tips for Dealing with Temptation:

- Satisfy your tooth with keto desserts sweetened with options like stevia or erythritol.
- Opt for water, herbal teas, or coffee with almond milk instead of reaching for sugary drinks.

### Carb Heavy Veggies

Vegetables You Should Avoid: Potatoes, potatoes, corn, peas.

Reasons to Skip Them: These starchy vegetables are rich in carbs. It can disrupt ketosis.

Here are some suggestions for overcoming challenges:

- Consider choosing vegetables not high in starch, such as cauliflower and broccoli.
- Try using cauliflower as an alternative to potatoes.

### Legumes

Foods to Steer Clear of Beans, lentils, and chickpeas.

Reasons for Avoiding Them: Legumes contain levels of carbohydrates, which may hinder your efforts to reach or sustain ketosis.

Tips for Overcoming Challenges:

- Opt for vegetables or nuts as protein-rich substitutes.
- Try out keto recipes that incorporate flour or coconut flour instead of legumes.

# Meal Planning and Preparation
## Tips for meal prepping

### 1. Organize Your Meals

Plan your weekly meals, covering breakfast, lunch, dinner, and snacks. Seek recipes aligning with your keto diet and establish a meal schedule. Ensure you incorporate a mix of proteins, healthy fats, and carb vegetables to maintain variety and excitement in your meals.

### 2. Compile a Shopping List

Once you have your meal plan in place, create a grocery list. Having a list will keep you on track during shopping trips. Ensure that you gather all items in one go. Stick to the store's sections where fresh produce, meats, and dairy are typically situated.

### 3. Prepare Proteins in Batches

Cook up quantities of proteins such as chicken, beef, or pork in advance. To streamline this process, you can utilize tools like cookers, Instant Pots, or ovens. After cooking them thoroughly, portion the proteins into containers designated for each meal. This way, you can quickly put together your meals throughout the week.

### 4. Prepare Your Vegetables

Start by washing, chopping, and storing your veggies in airtight containers. Spinach, broccoli, cauliflower, and bell peppers are choices for a keto diet and can be used in various dishes. Prepping them ahead of time saves time and makes it convenient to incorporate them into your meals.

### 5. Incorporate Healthy Fats

Include fats like avocado, olive oil, coconut oil, and nuts in your meal-prepping routine. These fats are vital for a keto lifestyle and help you feel satiated. Make guacamole or homemade dressings beforehand to add flavor and nutritious fats to your meals.

### 6. Manage Portion Sizes

When storing your meals, opt for containers that match portions. This practice helps you control serving sizes and prevent overeating. Remember to label the containers with the meal type and date for freshness tracking.

### 7. Utilize Your Freezer

Prepare meals that can be frozen for use. Soups, stews, and casseroles are choices here. Keeping meals on hand is a game changer on hectic days when cooking from scratch isn't an option.

### 8. Stick to Simplicity

Make sure your meal prep is simple enough. Focus on recipes that involve few ingredients or steps. This approach streamlines the process. It makes it more manageable.

### 9. Keep it Steady

Incorporate meal prepping into your schedule. Designate a week's day and time for planning, shopping, and prepping. Consistency plays a role in forming the habit of meal prepping.

### 10. Have Fun Along the Way

- Lastly, find joy in the process! Meal prepping can be a fulfilling activity. It empowers you to choose what you eat and keeps you dedicated to your keto diet objectives.

# How to Read Nutrition Labels: A Guide for Keto Beginners

## 1. Serving Size and Servings Per Container

When checking a nutrition label, look at the serving size and the number of servings per container. All the nutritional information is based on this serving size, so be mindful not to consume too many servings in one go, as this can significantly affect your nutrient intake.

## 2. Calories

After that, check the calories per serving. Even though the keto diet focuses more on macronutrients than calorie counting, it's still important to know your caloric intake to maintain a rounded diet and support your energy levels.

## 3. Total Carbohydrates

Those following a keto diet should pay attention to the carbohydrates on the label. This includes all carbohydrates, including fiber, sugars, and sugar alcohols. To calculate carbohydrates (the carbs affecting blood sugar levels), subtract fiber and a portion of sugar alcohols from the total carbohydrates. Keeping carbs low below 20-50 grams daily is crucial for staying in ketosis.

## 4. Dietary Fiber

Dietary fiber is a type of carbohydrate that your body can't digest. It doesn't raise blood sugar levels.

Consuming foods rich in fiber can help you feel satisfied and promote digestion. Ducting the fiber content from the carbohydrates is essential to determine the carbs.

## 5. Sugars and Added Sugars

When checking food labels, consider the sugar content, including added sugars. Foods high in sugars can cause spikes in blood glucose levels, which isn't ideal for a keto diet. Opt for products with added sugars to stay within your carb limit.

## 6. Sugar Alcohols

Certain keto-friendly items use sugar alcohols like erythritol or xylitol as sweeteners because they impact blood sugar levels. However, not all sugar alcohols are the same. Erythritol, for instance, affects blood sugar, whereas others may still contribute to your carb intake. Typically, you can subtract half of the grams of sugar alcohols from the carbs to calculate carbs.

## 7. Total Fat and Types of Fat

Considering that fats are a component of the keto diet, pay attention to both the fat content and the types of fats present in products. Focus on incorporating fats such as monounsaturated and polyunsaturated fats while limiting trans fats and saturated fats. Healthy fats play a role in supporting ketosis and providing energy.

## 8. Protein

Protein is another macronutrient that should be included in your keto diet plan.

- Consuming protein sparingly could disrupt ketosis. Ensure the item contains a level of protein that aligns with your macronutrient targets.

## 9. Ingredients List

Make sure to check the list of ingredients. The ingredients are usually arranged based on quantity, starting from the most to the least. Stay away from items containing sugars, processed carbs, and artificial additives. Opt for ingredients to ensure that the product meets the guidelines of the keto diet.

## 10. Vitamins and Minerals

While the keto diet mainly focuses on macronutrients, it's crucial to prioritize your health and well-being. Don't overlook the significance of vitamins and minerals. Look out for nutrients such as potassium, magnesium, and vitamins that play a key role in supporting bodily functions and maintaining good health.

Practical Tips for Reading Labels

- Approach Health Claims with Caution: Descriptions like 'carb,' 'keto-friendly,' or 'sugar-free' can sometimes be deceiving. But don't worry; it's easy to check these statements by reviewing both the nutritional information and ingredient list. This way, you can make informed choices without feeling overwhelmed. Compare Products: While shopping, compare items to select one that best fits your keto dietary requirements.

- Maintain a Shopping List: Keeping track of keto brands and products can simplify your grocery trips.

# CHAPTER 2:
# BREAKFAST RECIPES

# Berry Avocado Delight Smoothie

**PREPARATION:**
**10 minutes**

**SERVES**
**2**

## INGREDIENTS

- 1 ripe avocado
- 1/2 cup unsweetened almond milk
- 1/2 cup full-fat coconut milk
- 1/2 cup fresh or frozen mixed berries (blueberries, raspberries, strawberries)
- 2 tablespoons chia seeds
- 2 tablespoons MCT oil or coconut oil
- 1 teaspoon vanilla extract
- Stevia or monk fruit sweetener to taste
- Ice cubes (optional)

## COOKING PROCESS

1. Prepare Ingredients: Halve the avocado, remove the pit, and scoop the flesh into a blender.
2. Combine Ingredients: Add almond milk, coconut milk, mixed berries, chia seeds, MCT oil, vanilla extract, and sweetener to the blender.
3. Blend: Blend until smooth and creamy. Add ice cubes if a thicker consistency is desired.
4. Adjust Sweetness: Taste and adjust the sweetness if necessary.
5. Serve: Pour into glasses and enjoy immediately.

*Nutritional Information (Per Serving): Calories: 320  Protein: 4g  Net Carbs: 5g  Total Fat: 29g  Cholesterol: 0mg  Sodium: 40mg  Potassium: 550mg*

---

# Green Detox Keto Smoothie

**PREPARATION:**
**5 minutes**

**SERVES**
**2**

## INGREDIENTS

- 1 cup unsweetened almond milk
- 1/2 avocado
- 1 cup fresh spinach
- 1/4 cup full-fat coconut milk
- 1 tablespoon chia seeds
- 1 tablespoon powdered erythritol (optional)
- 1/2 teaspoon vanilla extract
- 1/2 cup ice cubes

Optional Garnish:
- Fresh mint leaves
- Lime wedge

## COOKING PROCESS

1. Blend: Combine almond milk, avocado, spinach, cucumber, chia seeds, MCT oil, lemon juice, ginger, and stevia in a blender.
2. Add Ice: Blend until smooth, then add ice cubes and blend again.
3. Taste & Adjust: Adjust sweetness with more stevia if needed.
4. Serve: Pour into glasses. Optionally garnish with mint leaves or a pinch of sea salt.

*Nutritional Information (Per Serving): Calories: 220  Protein: 4g  Net Carbohydrates: 3g  Fats: 20g  Fiber: 6g  Cholesterol: 0mg  Sodium: 80mg  Potassium: 450mg*

# Vanilla Almond Protein Smoothie

### PREPARATION
**5 minutes**

### SERVES
**2**

### INGREDIENTS

- 1 cup unsweetened almond milk
- 1/2 cup full-fat coconut milk
- 1/2 avocado
- 1 scoop vanilla protein powder (keto-friendly)
- 1 tbsp almond butter
- 1 tbsp MCT oil (or coconut oil)
- 1 tsp vanilla extract
- 2-3 drops liquid stevia
- 1 cup ice cubes
- Optional Ingredients:
- 1 tsp unsweetened shredded coconut
- A pinch of cinnamon
- A few drops of almond extract

### COOKING PROCESS

1. Blend: Combine almond milk, coconut milk, avocado, protein powder, almond butter, MCT oil, vanilla extract, and stevia in a blender.
2. Add Ice: Blend until smooth, then add ice cubes and blend again.
3. Taste & Adjust: Adjust sweetness with more stevia if needed.
4. Serve: Pour into glasses. Optionally garnish with shredded coconut, a pinch of cinnamon, or a few drops of almond extract.

*Nutritional Information (Per Serving): Calories: 320 Protein: 15g Net Carbs: 4g Fiber: 5g Fats: 28g Cholesterol: 0mg Sodium: 150mg Potassium: 450mg*

# Creamy Coconut Matcha Smoothie

### PREPARATION
**5 minutes**

### SERVES
**4**

### INGREDIENTS

- 1 cup full-fat coconut milk
- 1/2 cup unsweetened almond milk
- 1 tablespoon matcha green tea powder
- 2 tablespoons MCT oil (or coconut oil)
- 1/2 avocado
- 1 tablespoon chia seeds
- 1 teaspoon vanilla extract
- 2-3 drops liquid stevia (or to taste)
- 1 cup ice cubes

Optional Ingredients:

- 1 tsp unsweetened shredded coconut
- Mint leaves
- Pinch of cinnamon
- Drops of almond extract

### COOKING PROCESS

1. Blend Base Ingredients: In a blender, combine the full-fat coconut milk, unsweetened almond milk, matcha powder, MCT oil, avocado, chia seeds, vanilla extract, and liquid stevia.
2. Add Ice: Add the ice cubes and blend until smooth.
3. Taste & Adjust: Taste and add more stevia if needed for sweetness.
4. Serve: Pour into two glasses.
5. Optional Garnish: Garnish with unsweetened shredded coconut, mint leaves, a pinch of cinnamon, or a few drops of almond extract as desired.

*Nutritional Information (Per Serving): Calories: 320 Protein: 3g Net Carbs: 3g Fiber: 4g Fats: 32g Cholesterol: 0mg Sodium: 50mg Potassium: 350mg*

# Cheesy Spinach and Mushroom Keto Omelette

**Preparation Time: 10 minutes    Cooking Time: 10 minutes    Servings: 2**

## INGREDIENTS

- 4 large eggs
- 2 tbsp heavy cream
- 2 tbsp butter
- 1 cup fresh spinach, chopped
- 1/2 cup mushrooms, sliced
- 1/2 cup shredded mozzarella cheese
- 1/4 cup grated Parmesan cheese
- Salt and pepper to taste
- Optional: 1/4 tsp garlic powder, 1/4 tsp onion powder, fresh herbs (parsley or chives) for garnish

## COOKING PROCESS

1. Whisk eggs, heavy cream, salt, pepper, and optional garlic and onion powders in a bowl.
2. Sauté mushrooms in 1 tbsp butter over medium heat for 2-3 minutes. Add spinach and cook until wilted. Set aside.
3. Cook eggs in remaining butter until edges set (2-3 minutes).
4. Fill half the omelette with mozzarella, cooked spinach, mushrooms, and Parmesan.
5. Fold omelette and cook until cheese melts (1-2 minutes).

*Nutritional Information (Per Serving): Calories: 400  Protein: 22g  Carbs: 5g  Fat: 33g  Fiber: 1g*
*Cholesterol: 400mg  Sodium: 500mg  Potassium: 400mg*

---

# Bacon and Avocado Keto Egg Muffins

**Preparation: 10 minutes    Cooking: 20 minutes    Servings: 6 muffins**

## INGREDIENTS

- 6 large eggs
- 4 slices bacon, cooked and crumbled
- 1 avocado, diced
- 1/4 cup shredded cheddar cheese
- 1/4 cup heavy cream
- Salt and pepper to taste
- Optional: chopped chives for garnish

## COOKING PROCESS

1. Preheat Oven: Preheat to 375°F (190°C). Grease a muffin tin.
2. Prepare Egg Mixture: In a bowl, whisk together eggs, heavy cream, salt, and pepper.
3. Assemble Muffins: Divide crumbled bacon and diced avocado evenly among the muffin cups. Pour the egg mixture over the bacon and avocado, filling each cup about 3/4 full. Sprinkle shredded cheddar cheese on top.
4. Bake: Bake for 18-20 minutes, until the eggs are set and the tops are golden brown.
5. Serve: Let cool slightly before removing from the muffin tin. Garnish with chopped chives if desired. Serve warm.

*Nutritional Information (Per Serving): Calories: 220  Protein: 12g  Carbohydrates: 3g  Fats: 18g  Fiber: 1g*
*Cholesterol: 220mg  Sodium: 300mg  Potassium: 250mg*

# Creamy Garlic Parmesan Keto Scrambled Eggs
**Preparation: 5 minutes          Cooking: 10 minutes          Servings: 2**

## INGREDIENTS

- 4 large eggs
- 1/4 cup heavy cream
- 2 tablespoons butter
- 2 cloves garlic, minced
- 1/4 cup grated Parmesan cheese
- Salt and pepper to taste
- Optional: fresh parsley or chives for garnish

*Nutritional Information (Per Serving):*
*Calories: 330  Protein: 16g  Carbs: 3g*
*Fats: 28g  Fiber: 0g  Cholesterol: 350mg*
*Sodium: 450mg  Potassium: 200mg*

## COOKING PROCESS

1. Whisk Eggs: In a bowl, whisk together eggs, heavy cream, salt, and pepper.
2. Sauté Garlic: Melt butter in a skillet over medium-low heat. Add minced garlic and sauté for 1 minute.
3. Cook Eggs: Pour egg mixture into skillet. Stir constantly until eggs start to set but are still creamy.
4. Add Cheese: Sprinkle Parmesan over eggs and cook for another minute until cheese melts.
5. Serve: Garnish with parsley or chives if desired.

---

# Keto Eggs Benedict with Hollandaise Sauce
**Preparation: 15 minutes          Cooking: 15 minutes          Servings: 2**

## INGREDIENTS

Eggs Benedict:
- 4 large eggs
- 2 slices Canadian bacon or ham
- 2 keto-friendly English muffins (or 4 slices of keto bread)
- 1 tbsp white vinegar

Hollandaise Sauce:
- 3 large egg yolks
- 1/2 cup unsalted butter, melted
- 1 tbsp lemon juice
- Salt and pepper to taste
- Optional: pinch of cayenne or paprika

## COOKING PROCESS

1. Hollandaise Sauce: Whisk egg yolks and lemon juice in a heatproof bowl over simmering water. Slowly add melted butter while whisking until thickened. Season with salt and pepper. Keep warm.
2. Poach Eggs: Simmer water with vinegar. Crack eggs into small bowls and slide into water. Poach 3-4 minutes. Remove with a slotted spoon.
3. Toast Muffins: Toast keto muffins or bread slices until golden.
4. Cook Bacon: Heat bacon slices in a skillet until browned.
5. Assemble: Place bacon on toasted muffin halves, top with poached eggs, and spoon over hollandaise sauce. Garnish with cayenne or paprika.

*Nutritional Information (Per Serving): Calories: 450  Protein: 18g  Carbohydrates: 4g  Fats: 40g  Fiber: 2g*
*Cholesterol: 400mg  Sodium: 600mg  Potassium: 250mg*

# Scrambled Eggs with Spinach and Avocado

**Preparation: 5 minutes      Cooking: 5 minutes      Servings: 2**

## INGREDIENTS

- 4 large eggs
- 1/4 cup milk or unsweetened almond milk
- 1 cup fresh spinach, chopped
- 1 avocado, diced
- 2 tbsp butter or olive oil
- Salt and pepper to taste

## COOKING PROCESS

1. Whisk Eggs: In a bowl, whisk together eggs, milk, salt, and pepper.
2. Cook Spinach: In a skillet, heat butter or olive oil over medium heat. Add chopped spinach and cook until wilted.
3. Scramble Eggs: Pour the egg mixture into the skillet with spinach. Cook, stirring gently, until eggs are just set.
4. Add Avocado: Remove from heat and gently fold in the diced avocado.
5. Serve: Divide between plates and serve immediately.

*Nutritional Information (Per Serving): Calories: 250  Protein: 12g  Carbs: 6g  Fats: 20g  Fiber: 4g*
*Cholesterol: 340mg  Sodium: 200mg  Potassium: 600mg*

---

# Omelette with Tomatoes, Basil, and Mozzarella

**Preparation: 5 minutes      Cooking: 5 minutes      Servings: 1**

## INGREDIENTS

- 3 large eggs
- 1/4 cup cherry tomatoes, halved
- 1/4 cup fresh basil leaves, chopped
- 1/4 cup shredded mozzarella cheese
- 1 tbsp butter or olive oil
- Salt and pepper to taste

## COOKING PROCESS

1. Whisk Eggs: In a bowl, whisk eggs with salt and pepper.
2. Cook Eggs: Heat butter or olive oil in a non-stick skillet over medium heat. Pour in the eggs and let cook undisturbed until the edges start to set.
3. Add Fillings: Sprinkle cherry tomatoes, basil, and mozzarella cheese over one half of the omelette.
4. Fold Omelette: Fold the other half over the fillings. Cook for another minute until the cheese melts.
5. Serve: Slide onto a plate and serve immediately.

*Nutritional Information (Per Serving): Calories: 300  Protein: 18g  Carbs: 4g  Fats: 24g  Fiber: 1g*
*Cholesterol: 560mg  Sodium: 350mg  Potassium: 300mg*

# Coconut Flour Blueberry Keto Pancakes

**Preparation Time: 10 minutes     Cooking Time: 15 minutes     Servings: 4**

## INGREDIENTS

Dry:
- 1/2 cup coconut flour
- 1 tsp baking powder
- 1/4 tsp salt

Wet:
- 4 large eggs
- 1/4 cup unsweetened almond milk
- 1/4 cup melted coconut oil or butter
- 1 tsp vanilla extract
- 2 tbsp keto-friendly sweetener

Add-ins:
- 1/2 cup fresh or frozen blueberries

For Cooking:
- Butter or coconut oil for greasing

## COOKING PROCESS

1. Mix Dry Ingredients: Combine coconut flour, baking powder, and salt.
2. Mix Wet Ingredients: In another bowl, beat eggs and add almond milk, melted coconut oil, vanilla extract, and sweetener.
3. Combine: Gradually mix dry ingredients into wet until smooth. Fold in blueberries.
4. Cook: Heat and grease a skillet over medium-low heat. Pour 1/4 cup batter per pancake. Cook 2-3 minutes per side until golden brown.
5. Serve: Garnish with fresh blueberries, sugar-free syrup, or whipped cream.

*Nutritional Information (Per Serving): Calories: 250*
*Protein: 8g Carbohydrates: 11g Fats: 20g Cholesterol: 186mg*
*Sodium: 208mg Potassium: 105mg*

---

# Fluffy Almond Flour Keto Pancakes

**Preparation Time: 10 minutes   Cooking Time: 15 minutes   Servings: 4**

## INGREDIENTS

Dry Ingredients:
- 1 cup almond flour
- 2 tbsp coconut flour
- 2 tsp baking powder
- 1/4 tsp salt

Wet Ingredients:
- 3 large eggs
- 1/3 cup unsweetened almond milk
- 2 tbsp melted butter or coconut oil
- 1 tsp vanilla extract
- 1-2 tbsp erythritol (optional)

Optional Ingredients:
- 1/4 cup berries or nuts (optional)
- Butter or coconut oil for cooking
- Sugar-free syrup or fresh berries for serving

## COOKING PROCESS

1. Mix Dry Ingredients: Combine almond flour, coconut flour, baking powder, and salt.
2. Mix Wet Ingredients: Whisk eggs, then add almond milk, melted butter, vanilla extract, and erythritol.
3. Combine: Mix wet and dry ingredients until smooth. Adjust thickness with more almond milk if needed.
4. Cook Pancakes: Heat a greased non-stick skillet over medium heat. Pour 1/4 cup batter per pancake, add optional berries/nuts. Cook until bubbles form, flip, and cook until golden brown.
5. Serve: Top with sugar-free syrup or fresh berries.

*Nutritional Information (Per Serving): Calories: 310 Protein: 12g Carbohydrates: 6g Fiber: 3g*
*Fat: 27g Cholesterol: 120mg Sodium: 280mg Potassium: 140mg*

# Cream Cheese Keto Pancakes

**Prep Time: 5 minutes     Cook Time: 10 minutes     Servings: 4**

## INGREDIENTS

- 4 oz cream cheese, softened
- 4 large eggs
- 1/2 tsp vanilla extract
- 2 tbsp keto sweetener
- 1/2 tsp baking powder
- 1/4 cup almond flour
- Butter or coconut oil for cooking

## COOKING PROCESS

1. Blend Batter: Mix cream cheese, eggs, vanilla, and sweetener until smooth. Add baking powder and almond flour, blend until smooth.
2. Cook: Heat and grease a skillet over medium heat. Pour 2-3 tbsp batter per pancake. Cook 2-3 minutes each side until golden brown.
3. Serve: Garnish with berries, sugar-free syrup, or whipped cream.

*Nutritional Information (Per Serving): Calories: 250  Protein: 9g  Carbs: 4g  Fats: 22g*
*Cholesterol: 189mg Sodium: 210mg  Potassium: 100mg*

---

# Lemon Ricotta Keto Pancakes

**Prep Time: 10 minutes     Cook Time: 10 minutes     Servings: 4**

## INGREDIENTS

- 1/2 cup almond flour
- 1/4 cup coconut flour
- 1 tsp baking powder
- 1/4 tsp salt
- 3 large eggs
- 1/2 cup ricotta cheese
- 1/4 cup unsweetened almond milk
- 2 tbsp keto sweetener
- 1 tsp vanilla extract
- Zest of 1 lemon
- 2 tbsp lemon juice
- Butter or coconut oil for cooking

Optional Garnish:
- Fresh berries
- Sugar-free syrup
- Lemon zest

## COOKING PROCESS

1. Mix Dry Ingredients: Combine almond flour, coconut flour, baking powder, and salt in a bowl.
2. Mix Wet Ingredients: In another bowl, whisk eggs, ricotta cheese, almond milk, sweetener, vanilla extract, lemon zest, and lemon juice until smooth.
3. Combine: Gradually mix dry ingredients into wet ingredients until well combined.
4. Cook Pancakes: Heat and grease a skillet over medium heat. Pour 2-3 tbsp batter per pancake. Cook 2-3 minutes each side until golden brown.
5. Serve: Garnish with fresh berries, sugar-free syrup, or extra lemon zest.

*Nutritional Information (Per Serving): Calories: 230  Protein: 10g  Carbs: 7g  Fats: 19g*
*Cholesterol: 170mg  Sodium: 210mg  Potassium: 110mg*

# Cinnamon Vanilla Keto Waffles

**Prep Time: 10 minutes    Cook Time: 15 minutes    Servings: 4**

## INGREDIENTS

- 2 cups almond flour
- 1/4 cup coconut flour
- 1 tsp baking powder
- 1/2 tsp salt
- 1 tsp ground cinnamon

- 4 large eggs
- 1/4 cup melted butter or coconut oil
- 1/4 cup unsweetened almond milk
- 2 tbsp keto sweetener
- 1 tsp vanilla extract

Optional Garnish:
- Sugar-free syrup
- Fresh berries
- Whipped cream (sugar-free)
- Extra cinnamon sprinkle

## COOKING PROCESS

1. Mix Dry Ingredients: Combine almond flour, coconut flour, baking powder, salt, and cinnamon in a bowl.
2. Mix Wet Ingredients: In another bowl, whisk eggs, melted butter, almond milk, sweetener, and vanilla extract until smooth.
3. Combine: Gradually mix dry ingredients into wet ingredients until well combined.
4. Cook Waffles: Preheat and grease a waffle iron. Pour batter into the waffle iron and cook according to the manufacturer's instructions until golden brown and crispy.

*Nutritional Information (Per Serving): Calories: 310  Protein: 12g  Carbs: 8g  Fats: 27g*
*Cholesterol: 185mg  Sodium: 320mg  Potassium: 150mg*

---

# Crispy Almond Flour Keto Waffles

**Prep Time: 10 minutes    Cook Time: 15 minutes    Servings: 4**

## INGREDIENTS

- 2 cups almond flour
- 1/4 cup coconut flour
- 1 tsp baking powder
- 1/2 tsp salt
- 4 large eggs

- 1/4 cup melted butter or coconut oil
- 1/4 cup unsweetened almond milk
- 2 tbsp keto sweetener
- 1 tsp vanilla extract

Optional Garnish:
- Sugar-free syrup
- Fresh berries
- Whipped cream (sugar-free)

## COOKING PROCESS

1. Mix Dry Ingredients: Combine almond flour, coconut flour, baking powder, and salt in a bowl.
2. Mix Wet Ingredients: In another bowl, whisk eggs, melted butter, almond milk, sweetener, and vanilla extract until smooth.
3. Combine: Gradually mix dry ingredients into wet ingredients until well combined.
4. Cook Waffles: Preheat and grease a waffle iron. Pour batter into the waffle iron and cook according to the manufacturer's instructions until golden brown and crispy.
5. Serve: Optional top with sugar-free syrup, fresh berries, or whipped cream.

*Nutritional Information (Per Serving): Calories: 300  Protein: 12g  Carbs: 8g  Fats: 26g*
*Cholesterol: 185mg  Sodium: 320mg  Potassium: 150mg*

# Chocolate Hazelnut Keto Waffles

**Prep Time: 10 minutes     Cook Time: 15 minutes     Servings: 4**

## INGREDIENTS

- 2 cups almond flour
- 1/4 cup hazelnut flour
- 1/4 cup cocoa powder
- 1 tsp baking powder
- 1/2 tsp salt
- 4 large eggs
- 1/4 cup melted butter
- 1/4 cup unsweetened almond milk
- 2 tbsp keto sweetener
- 1 tsp vanilla extract
- 1/4 cup chopped hazelnuts (optional)

## COOKING PROCESS

1. Mix Batter: Combine dry ingredients: almond flour, hazelnut flour, cocoa powder, baking powder, and salt. Whisk wet ingredients: eggs, melted butter, almond milk, sweetener, and vanilla. Mix dry into wet ingredients. Fold in chopped hazelnuts if using.

2. Cook Waffles: Preheat and grease a waffle iron. Pour batter into the waffle iron and cook until golden brown and crispy, about 3-5 minutes per waffle.

3. Serve: Optional Top with sugar-free chocolate syrup, whipped cream, or extra chopped hazelnuts.

*Nutritional Information (Per Serving): Calories: 320  Protein: 12g  Carbs: 10g  Fats: 28g*
*Cholesterol: 185mg  Sodium: 320mg  Potassium: 180mg*

---

# Cheddar Chive Savory Keto Waffles

**Prep Time: 10 minutes     Cook Time: 15 minutes     Servings: 4**

## INGREDIENTS

- 2 cups almond flour
- 1/4 cup coconut flour
- 1 tsp baking powder
- 1/2 tsp salt
- 1 tsp garlic powder
- 4 large eggs
- 1/4 cup melted butter
- 1/4 cup unsweetened almond milk
- 1 cup shredded cheddar cheese
- 1/4 cup chopped fresh chives

Optional Garnish:
- Sour cream
- Extra shredded cheddar cheese
- Extra chopped chives

## COOKING PROCESS

1. Mix Dry Ingredients: In a large bowl, combine almond flour, coconut flour, baking powder, salt, and garlic powder.

2. Mix Wet Ingredients: In another bowl, whisk eggs, melted butter, and almond milk until smooth.

3. Combine: Gradually mix dry ingredients into wet ingredients until well combined.Fold in shredded cheddar cheese and chopped chives.

4. Cook Waffles: Preheat and grease a waffle iron. Pour batter into the waffle iron and cook according to the manufacturer's instructions until golden brown and crispy, about 3-5 minutes per waffle.

*Nutritional Information (Per Serving): Calories: 340  Protein: 14g  Carbs: 8g*
*Fats: 29g  Cholesterol: 190mg  Sodium: 350mg  Potassium: 160mg*

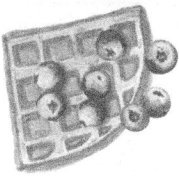

# Blueberry Coconut Keto Waffles

**Prep Time: 10 minutes     Cook Time: 10 minutes     Servings: 4**

## INGREDIENTS

- 1 cup almond flour
- 1/4 cup coconut flour
- 1/2 cup unsweetened shredded coconut
- 1 tsp baking powder
- 1/4 tsp salt
- 3 large eggs
- 1/4 cup coconut oil, melted
- 1/2 cup unsweetened almond milk
- 1 tbsp erythritol
- 1/2 cup fresh blueberries

## COOKING PROCESS

1. Preheat Waffle Iron.
2. Mix Dry Ingredients: Combine almond flour, coconut flour, shredded coconut, baking powder, and salt.
3. Mix Wet Ingredients: Whisk together eggs, melted coconut oil, almond milk, and erythritol.
4. Combine: Add wet to dry ingredients. Fold in blueberries.
5. Cook Waffles: Pour batter into waffle iron and cook until golden brown.
6. Serve: Serve hot with keto-friendly toppings.

*Nutritional Information (Per Serving): Calories: 250 Protein: 8g Carbs: 10g Fats: 20g Fiber: 5g*
*Cholesterol: 80mg Sodium: 200mg Potassium: 100mg*

---

# Pumpkin Spice Keto Waffles

**Prep Time: 10 minutes     Cook Time: 10 minutes     Servings: 4**

## INGREDIENTS

- 1 cup almond flour
- 1/4 cup coconut flour
- 1 tsp baking powder
- 1/4 tsp salt
- 1 tsp pumpkin pie spice
- 3 large eggs
- 1/2 cup pumpkin puree
- 1/4 cup coconut oil, melted
- 1/2 cup unsweetened almond milk
- 1 tbsp erythritol

## COOKING PROCESS

1. Preheat Waffle Iron.
2. Mix Dry Ingredients: Combine almond flour, coconut flour, baking powder, salt, and pumpkin pie spice.
3. Mix Wet Ingredients: Whisk together eggs, pumpkin puree, melted coconut oil, almond milk, and erythritol.
4. Combine: Add wet ingredients to dry ingredients and mix until well combined.
5. Cook Waffles: Pour batter into the waffle iron and cook until golden brown.
6. Serve: Serve hot with keto-friendly toppings.

*Nutritional Information (Per Serving): Calories: 230 Protein: 7g Carbs: 8g Fats: 19g Fiber: 4g*
*Cholesterol: 70mg Sodium: 200mg Potassium: 100mg*

# Spinach, Bacon, and Feta Keto Breakfast Bake

**Prep Time: 15 minutes      Cook Time: 35 minutes      Servings: 6**

## INGREDIENTS

- 8 slices bacon
- 6 large eggs
- 1/2 cup heavy cream
- 1 cup fresh spinach, chopped
- 1/2 cup crumbled feta cheese
- 1 cup shredded mozzarella cheese
- 1/4 cup chopped green onions
- 1/2 tsp garlic powder
- Salt and pepper to taste

## COOKING PROCESS

1. Preheat Oven: Preheat oven to 375°F (190°C).
2. Cook Bacon: In a skillet, cook bacon over medium heat until crispy. Remove and crumble the bacon.
3. Prepare Egg Mixture: In a large bowl, whisk together eggs, heavy cream, garlic powder, salt, and pepper.
4. Assemble Bake: In a greased 9x13 inch baking dish, spread chopped spinach evenly. Sprinkle with crumbled bacon, feta cheese, mozzarella cheese, and green onions. Pour the egg mixture over the top.
5. Bake: Bake in the preheated oven for 30-35 minutes, or until the eggs are set and the top is golden brown.

*Nutritional Information (Per Serving): Calories: 350 Protein: 18g Carbs: 4g Fats: 30g*

*Cholesterol: 240mg Sodium: 700mg Potassium: 250mg*

---

# Sausage and Cheese Keto Breakfast Casserole

**Prep Time: 15 minutes      Cook Time: 40 minutes      Servings: 6**

## INGREDIENTS

- 1 lb ground sausage
- 8 large eggs
- 1/2 cup heavy cream
- 1 cup shredded cheddar cheese
- 1 cup shredded mozzarella cheese
- 1/4 cup chopped green onions
- 1/2 tsp garlic powder
- 1/2 tsp onion powder
- Salt and pepper to taste

## COOKING PROCESS

1. Preheat Oven: Preheat oven to 375°F (190°C).
2. Cook Sausage: In a skillet, cook the ground sausage over medium heat until browned. Drain excess fat.
3. Prepare Egg Mixture: In a large bowl, whisk together eggs, heavy cream, garlic powder, onion powder, salt, and pepper.
4. Assemble Casserole: In a greased 9x13 inch baking dish, spread cooked sausage evenly. Sprinkle with cheddar cheese, mozzarella cheese, and green onions. Pour the egg mixture over the top.
5. Bake: Bake in the preheated oven for 35-40 minutes, or until the eggs are set and the top is golden brown.

*Nutritional Information (Per Serving): Calories: 400 Protein: 25g Carbs: 4g Fats: 32g Cholesterol: 250mg*

*Sodium: 800mg Potassium: 300mg*

# Mushroom and Swiss Keto Breakfast Casserole

**Prep Time: 15 minutes     Cook Time: 45 minutes     Servings: 6**

## INGREDIENTS

- 1 tbsp olive oil
- 1 cup sliced mushrooms
- 8 large eggs
- 1/2 cup heavy cream
- 1 cup shredded Swiss cheese
- 1/4 cup grated Parmesan cheese
- 1/2 cup chopped green onions
- 1/2 tsp garlic powder
- 1/2 tsp onion powder
- Salt and pepper to taste

## COOKING PROCESS

1. Preheat Oven: Preheat oven to 375°F (190°C).
2. Cook Mushrooms: In a skillet, heat olive oil over medium heat. Add mushrooms and cook until soft, about 5 minutes.
3. Prepare Egg Mixture: In a large bowl, whisk together eggs, heavy cream, garlic powder, onion powder, salt, and pepper.
4. Assemble Casserole: In a greased 9x13 inch baking dish, spread cooked mushrooms evenly. Sprinkle with Swiss cheese, Parmesan cheese, and green onions. Pour the egg mixture over the top.
5. Bake: Bake in the preheated oven for 35-40 minutes, or until the eggs are set and the top is golden brown.

*Nutritional Information (Per Serving):  Calories: 330  Protein: 18g  Carbs: 5g  Fats: 28g*
*Cholesterol: 240mg  Sodium: 600mg  Potassium: 300mg*

---

# Mexican Chorizo and Egg Keto Breakfast Casserole

**Prep Time: 15 minutes     Cook Time: 40 minutes     Servings: 6**

## INGREDIENTS

- 1 lb Mexican chorizo, casing removed
- 8 large eggs
- 1/2 cup heavy cream
- 1 cup shredded cheddar cheese
- 1 cup shredded Monterey Jack cheese
- 1/2 cup chopped bell peppers
- 1/2 cup chopped onions
- 1/4 cup chopped fresh cilantro
- 1/2 tsp cumin
- 1/2 tsp chili powder
- Salt and pepper to taste

Optional Garnish:
- Sliced avocado
- Salsa
- Sour cream

## COOKING PROCESS

1. Preheat Oven: 375°F (190°C).
2. Cook Chorizo: In a skillet, cook chorizo over medium heat until fully cooked. Drain excess fat.
3. Prepare Egg Mixture: In a bowl, whisk eggs, heavy cream, cumin, chili powder, salt, and pepper.
4. Assemble Casserole: In a greased 9x13 inch baking dish, spread cooked chorizo, bell peppers, onions, and cilantro. Sprinkle with cheeses. Pour egg mixture over the top.
5. Bake: 35-40 minutes, until eggs are set and top is golden brown.
6. Serve: Garnish with avocado, salsa, and sour cream if desired.

*Nutritional Information (Per Serving): Calories: 420  Protein: 22g  Carbs: 6g  Fats: 35g  Cholesterol: 250mg*
*Sodium: 900mg  Potassium: 400mg*

# Bacon and Broccoli Breakfast Bake

### Prep Time: 10 minutes    Cook Time: 30 minutes    Servings: 6

## INGREDIENTS

- 8 slices bacon, cooked and crumbled
- 2 cups broccoli florets, steamed
- 8 large eggs
- 1/2 cup heavy cream
- 1 cup shredded cheddar cheese
- 1/2 tsp garlic powder
- 1/2 tsp onion powder
- Salt and pepper to taste

## COOKING PROCESS

1. Preheat Oven: Preheat to 375°F (190°C). Grease a baking dish.
2. Prepare Bacon and Broccoli: Cook bacon until crispy and crumble. Steam broccoli florets until tender.
3. Mix Ingredients: In a bowl, whisk together eggs, heavy cream, garlic powder, onion powder, salt, and pepper. Stir in cooked bacon, steamed broccoli, and shredded cheddar cheese.
4. Bake: Pour the mixture into the greased baking dish. Bake for 25-30 minutes or until the eggs are set and the top is golden brown.
5. Serve: Let cool slightly before serving.

*Nutritional Information (Per Serving):  Calories: 300  Protein: 18g  Carbs: 3g  Fats: 24g  Fiber: 1g*
*Cholesterol: 250mg  Sodium: 450mg  Potassium: 300mg*

---

# Southwestern Keto Breakfast Casserole

### Prep Time: 10 minutes    Cook Time: 30 minutes    Servings: 6

## INGREDIENTS

- 1 lb ground sausage or beef
- 1 red bell pepper, diced
- 1 green bell pepper, diced
- 1/2 cup diced onions
- 1 cup shredded cheddar cheese
- 8 large eggs
- 1/2 cup heavy cream
- 1 tsp ground cumin
- 1 tsp chili powder
- Salt and pepper to taste

## COOKING PROCESS

1. Preheat Oven: Preheat to 375°F (190°C). Grease a baking dish.
2. Cook Meat and Vegetables: In a skillet, cook the ground sausage or beef over medium heat until browned. Add diced bell peppers and onions, and cook until vegetables are tender.
3. Mix Ingredients: In a bowl, whisk together eggs, heavy cream, cumin, chili powder, garlic powder, salt, and pepper. Stir in the cooked sausage mixture and shredded cheddar cheese.
4. Bake: Pour the mixture into the greased baking dish. Bake for 25-30 minutes or until the eggs are set and the top is golden brown.
5. Serve: Let cool slightly before serving. Garnish with chopped cilantro, sliced jalapeños, and avocado slices if desired.

*Nutritional Information (Per Serving): Calories: 350  Protein: 20g  Carbs: 5g  Fats: 28g  Fiber: 2g*
*Cholesterol: 250mg  Sodium: 600mg  Potassium: 350mg*

# Bacon-Wrapped Avocado Bites

**Prep Time: 10 minutes**     **Cook Time: 15 minutes**     **Servings: 2**

## INGREDIENTS

- 2 ripe avocados
- 12 slices of bacon
- 1/2 tsp garlic powder
- 1/2 tsp paprika
- Salt and pepper to taste
- Toothpicks

## COOKING PROCESS

1. Preheat Oven: 400°F (200°C).
2. Prepare Avocados: Cut avocados into 12 wedges. Sprinkle with garlic powder, paprika, salt, and pepper.
3. Wrap with Bacon: Wrap each avocado wedge with a slice of bacon and secure with a toothpick.
4. Bake: Place on a baking sheet lined with parchment paper. Bake for 12-15 minutes, until bacon is crispy.
5. Serve: Enjoy warm.

*Nutritional Information (Per Serving): Calories: 120  Protein: 4g  Carbs: 2g  Fats: 11g*
*Cholesterol: 15mg  Sodium: 190mg  Potassium: 200mg*

---

# Keto Avocado Bacon Egg Salad

**Prep Time: 15 minutes**     **Cook Time: 10 minutes**     **Servings: 4**

## INGREDIENTS

- 6 large eggs
- 2 ripe avocados, diced
- 6 slices bacon, cooked and crumbled
- 1/4 cup mayonnaise
- 1 tbsp Dijon mustard
- 1 tbsp lemon juice
- 1/4 cup chopped green onions
- Salt and pepper to taste

## COOKING PROCESS

1. Boil Eggs:  Place eggs in a pot, cover with water, and bring to a boil. Cook for 10 minutes. Cool, peel, and chop.
2. Prepare Salad:  In a large bowl, combine chopped eggs, diced avocados, crumbled bacon, and green onions.
3. Make Dressing:  In a small bowl, mix mayonnaise, Dijon mustard, lemon juice, salt, and pepper.
4. Combine:  Pour dressing over the salad and gently mix until well combined.
5. Serve: Enjoy immediately or refrigerate for later.

*Nutritional Information (Per Serving): Calories: 350  Protein: 12g  Carbs: 4g  Fats: 30g  Cholesterol: 210mg*
*Sodium: 400mg  Potassium: 400mg*

# Keto BLT Avocado Bowls

**Prep Time: 10 minutes      Cook Time: 10 minutes      Servings: 4**

## INGREDIENTS

- 4 large avocados, halved and pitted
- 8 slices bacon, cooked and crumbled
- 1 cup cherry tomatoes, halved
- 1/2 cup shredded lettuce
- 1/4 cup mayonnaise
- 1 tbsp lemon juice
- Salt and pepper to taste

## COOKING PROCESS

1. Prepare Avocados:  Scoop out a small portion of the avocado to create a larger cavity.
2. Mix Filling:  In a bowl, combine crumbled bacon, cherry tomatoes, shredded lettuce, mayonnaise, lemon juice, salt, and pepper.
3. Assemble Bowls: Fill each avocado half with the bacon, lettuce, and tomato mixture.
4. Serve: Enjoy immediately.

*Nutritional Information (Per Serving): Calories: 320  Protein: 10g  Carbs: 8g Fats: 28g Cholesterol: 25mg  Sodium: 450mg  Potassium: 600mg*

---

# Creamy Avocado and Bacon Zoodles

**Prep Time: 15 minutes      Cook Time: 10 minutes      Servings: 4**

## INGREDIENTS

- 4 medium zucchinis, spiralized
- 2 ripe avocados
- 6 slices bacon, cooked and crumbled
- 1/2 cup heavy cream
- 1/4 cup grated Parmesan cheese
- 1 tbsp lemon juice
- 2 cloves garlic, minced
- Salt and pepper to taste
- 2 tbsp olive oil

## COOKING PROCESS

1. Prepare Zoodles: Spiralize the zucchinis into noodles.
2. Make Avocado Sauce: In a blender, combine avocados, heavy cream, Parmesan cheese, lemon juice, garlic, salt, and pepper. Blend until smooth.
3. Cook Zoodles: In a large skillet, heat olive oil over medium heat. Add zoodles and cook for 2-3 minutes until slightly tender.
4. Combine: Add the avocado sauce to the skillet with zoodles. Toss to coat evenly and heat through for about 2 minutes.
5. Serve: Top with crumbled bacon and extra Parmesan if desired. Serve immediately.

*Nutritional Information (Per Serving): Calories: 350  Protein: 10g  Carbs: 8g  Fats: 30g Cholesterol: 45mg Sodium: 500mg  Potassium: 700mg*

# Avocado Bacon Deviled Eggs

**Prep Time: 10 minutes**     **Cook Time: 0 minutes**     **Servings: 12**

## INGREDIENTS

- 6 large eggs, hard-boiled and peeled
- 1 ripe avocado
- 3 slices bacon, cooked and crumbled
- 2 tbsp mayonnaise
- 1 tsp Dijon mustard
- 1 tsp lemon juice
- Salt and pepper to taste
- Optional: paprika for garnish

## COOKING PROCESS

1. Prepare Eggs: Slice the hard-boiled eggs in half lengthwise. Remove the yolks and place them in a bowl.
2. Mix Filling: Add avocado, mayonnaise, Dijon mustard, lemon juice, salt, and pepper to the bowl with the yolks. Mash and mix until smooth. Stir in crumbled bacon.
3. Fill Eggs: Spoon the avocado mixture into the egg whites.
4. Garnish: Sprinkle with paprika if desired.
5. Serve: Serve immediately or refrigerate until ready to serve.

*Nutritional Information (Per Serving): Calories: 90  Protein: 4g  Carbs: 1g  Fats: 8g  Fiber: 1g*
*Cholesterol: 80mg  Sodium: 100mg  Potassium: 150mg*

---

# Stuffed Avocados with Bacon and Cheese

**Prep Time: 10 minutes**     **Cook Time: 10 minutes**     **Servings: 4**

## INGREDIENTS

- 2 ripe avocados
- 4 slices bacon, cooked and crumbled
- 1/2 cup shredded cheddar cheese
- 1/4 cup sour cream
- 1/4 cup diced tomatoes
- 2 tbsp chopped green onions
- Salt and pepper to taste

## COOKING PROCESS

1. Prepare Avocados: Cut avocados in half and remove the pits. Scoop out some of the flesh to create a larger cavity.
2. Mix Filling: In a bowl, combine crumbled bacon, cheddar cheese, sour cream, diced tomatoes, green onions, salt, and pepper.
3. Stuff Avocados: Spoon the bacon and cheese mixture into the avocado halves.
4. Serve: Serve immediately.

*Nutritional Information (Per Serving): Calories: 250  Protein: 9g  Carbs: 8g  Fats: 21g  Fiber: 7g*
*Cholesterol: 25mg  Sodium: 300mg  Potassium: 500mg*

# CHAPTER 3: LUNCH RECIPES

# Avocado and Bacon Keto Cobb Salad

**Prep Time: 15 minutes    Cook Time: 10 minutes    Servings: 4**

## INGREDIENTS

- 6 slices bacon, cooked and crumbled
- 4 large eggs, hard-boiled and chopped
- 1 large avocado, diced
- 2 cups mixed greens
- 1 cup cherry tomatoes, halved
- 1/2 cup blue cheese crumbles
- 1/2 cup cooked chicken breast, diced
- 1/4 cup red onion, thinly sliced
- Dressing:
- 1/4 cup olive oil
- 2 tbsp red wine vinegar
- 1 tsp Dijon mustard
- 1 clove garlic, minced
- Salt and pepper to taste

## COOKING PROCESS

1. Prepare Ingredients: Cook and crumble the bacon. Hard-boil the eggs and chop. Dice the avocado and chicken breast. Halve the cherry tomatoes and thinly slice the red onion.
2. Make Dressing: In a small bowl, whisk together olive oil, red wine vinegar, Dijon mustard, garlic, salt, and pepper.
3. Assemble Salad: In a large bowl, layer mixed greens, cherry tomatoes, avocado, hard-boiled eggs, bacon, blue cheese crumbles, chicken, and red onion.

*Nutritional Information (Per Serving):  Calories: 450  Protein: 20g  Carbs: 10g  Fats: 38g*
*Cholesterol: 220mg  Sodium: 700mg  Potassium: 700mg*

---

# Grilled Chicken Caesar Keto Salad

**Prep Time: 15 minutes    Cook Time: 15 minutes    Servings: 4**

## INGREDIENTS

- 2 large chicken breasts
- 4 cups Romaine lettuce, chopped
- 1/2 cup grated Parmesan cheese
- 1/4 cup Caesar dressing (keto-friendly)
- 1 avocado, sliced
- 1/4 cup bacon bits (optional)
- Salt and pepper to taste

## COOKING PROCESS

1. Grill Chicken: Season chicken breasts with salt and pepper. Grill over medium heat for 6-7 minutes per side, or until fully cooked. Let rest and slice.
2. Assemble Salad: In a large bowl, combine chopped Romaine lettuce, Parmesan cheese, and bacon bits if using.
3. Add Chicken and Avocado: Top salad with grilled chicken slices and avocado.
4. Dress and Serve: Drizzle with Caesar dressing and toss gently before serving.

*Nutritional Information (Per Serving): Calories: 400  Protein: 30g  Carbs: 6g Fats: 28g Cholesterol: 100mg*
*Sodium: 750mg  Potassium: 600mg*

# Spinach and Feta Keto Greek Salad

**Prep Time: 15 minutes**    **Cook Time: 0 minutes**    **Servings: 4**

## INGREDIENTS

- 4 cups fresh spinach, chopped
- 1 cup cherry tomatoes, halved
- 1/2 cup cucumber, diced
- 1/2 cup red onion, thinly sliced
- 1/2 cup Kalamata olives, pitted and halved
- 1/2 cup crumbled feta cheese
- 1/4 cup olive oil
- 2 tbsp red wine vinegar
- 1 tsp dried oregano
- Salt and pepper to taste

## COOKING PROCESS

1. Prepare Vegetables: In a large bowl, combine chopped spinach, cherry tomatoes, cucumber, red onion, and Kalamata olives.
2. Add Feta: Sprinkle crumbled feta cheese over the salad.
3. Make Dressing: In a small bowl, whisk together olive oil, red wine vinegar, oregano, salt, and pepper.
4. Dress and Serve: Drizzle dressing over the salad and toss gently before serving.

*Nutritional Information (Per Serving): Calories: 200 Protein: 5g Carbs: 6g Fats: 18g*
*Cholesterol: 15mg Sodium: 450mg Potassium: 450mg*

---

# Tuna and Egg Keto Salad with Lemon Dressing

**Prep Time: 15 minutes**    **Cook Time: 10 minutes**    **Servings: 4**

## INGREDIENTS

Salad:
- 2 cans (5 oz each) tuna in olive oil, drained
- 4 large eggs, hard-boiled and chopped
- 1 avocado, diced
- 1 cup cherry tomatoes, halved
- 1/2 cup cucumber, diced
- 1/4 cup red onion, finely chopped
- 1/4 cup black olives, sliced
- 2 cups fresh spinach or mixed greens

Lemon Dressing:
- 1/4 cup extra virgin olive oil
- 2 tbsp lemon juice
- 1 tsp Dijon mustard
- 1 clove garlic, minced
- 1/2 tsp salt
- 1/4 tsp black pepper

Optional Garnish:
- 1 tbsp fresh dill, chopped
- 1 tbsp fresh parsley, chopped
- 1/4 tsp red pepper flakes

## COOKING PROCESS

1. Hard-Boil Eggs: Boil eggs for 9-12 minutes, cool in ice water, peel and chop.
2. Prepare Salad: Mix tuna, avocado, tomatoes, cucumber, red onion, olives, and chopped eggs in a bowl.
3. Make Dressing: Whisk olive oil, lemon juice, mustard, garlic, salt, and pepper.
4. Assemble: Toss salad with dressing. Serve over spinach or greens. Garnish as desired.

*Nutritional Information (Per Serving): Calories: 320 Protein: 22g Carbs: 6g Fats: 24g Fiber: 4g Cholesterol: 225mg Sodium: 550mg Potassium: 500mg*

# Creamy Broccoli Cheddar Keto Soup

**Prep Time: 10 minutes     Cook Time: 20 minutes     Servings: 4**

## INGREDIENTS

- 4 cups broccoli florets
- 1 cup heavy cream
- 2 cups chicken broth
- 1 cup sharp cheddar cheese, shredded
- 1/2 cup grated Parmesan cheese
- 1/4 cup butter
- 1 small onion, finely chopped
- 2 cloves garlic, minced
- Salt and pepper to taste
- Optional garnish: extra shredded cheddar, chopped parsley

## COOKING PROCESS

1. Cook Broccoli: Steam or boil the broccoli florets until tender (about 5-7 minutes). Set aside.
2. Sauté Aromatics: In a large pot, melt the butter over medium heat. Add the chopped onion and garlic, sauté until softened (about 3-4 minutes).
3. Add Broth and Cream: Pour in the chicken broth and heavy cream. Bring to a simmer.
4. Blend: Add the cooked broccoli to the pot. Use an immersion blender to puree the mixture until smooth. Alternatively, blend in batches in a regular blender.
5. Add Cheese: Stir in the shredded cheddar and Parmesan cheese until melted and well combined. Season with salt and pepper to taste.

*Nutritional Information (Per Serving): Calories: 340  Protein: 14g  Carbohydrates: 6g  Fats: 29g  Fiber: 2g*
*Cholesterol: 85mg  Sodium: 750mg  Potassium: 450mg*

---

# Keto Chicken and Mushroom Soup

**Prep Time: 10 minutes     Cook Time: 25 minutes     Servings: 4**

## INGREDIENTS

- 2 cups sliced mushrooms (such as cremini or button mushrooms)
- 1 small onion, finely chopped
- 2 cloves garlic, minced
- 4 cups chicken broth
- 1 cup heavy cream
- 1/4 cup butter
- 1 tsp dried thyme
- 1 tsp dried rosemary
- Salt and pepper to taste
- Optional garnish: chopped fresh parsley

## COOKING PROCESS

1. Cook Chicken: Sauté chicken in butter until browned and cooked through. Remove from pot
2. Cook Veggies: Sauté onion and garlic in the same pot until soft. Add mushrooms and cook until tender.
3. Simmer: Add chicken broth, thyme, and rosemary. Simmer.
4. Combine: Return chicken to pot, stir in heavy cream, and simmer for 10 minutes.
5. Serve: Season with salt and pepper. Garnish with parsley if desired.

*Nutritional Information (Per Serving): Calories: 320  Protein: 22g  Carbs: 5g  Fats: 24g  Fiber: 1g*
*Cholesterol: 110mg  Sodium: 800mg  Potassium: 600mg*

# Rich and Creamy Tomato Basil Keto Soup

**Prep Time: 10 minutes**     **Cook Time: 20 minutes**     **Servings: 4**

## INGREDIENTS

- 1 lb shrimp, peeled and deveined
- 1 tbsp olive oil
- 2 cloves garlic, minced
- 1 tsp chili powder
- 1/2 tsp paprika
- 1/2 tsp cumin
- 1/4 tsp cayenne pepper
- Salt and pepper to taste
- 8 large lettuce leaves
- 1 avocado, sliced
- 1/2 cup cherry tomatoes, halved
- 1/4 cup red onion, thinly sliced
- 1/4 cup fresh cilantro, chopped
- Optional: lime wedges

## COOKING PROCESS

1. Season Shrimp: Toss shrimp with olive oil, garlic, and spices.
2. Cook Shrimp: Sauté shrimp in a skillet over medium-high heat for 2-3 minutes per side until cooked through.
3. Assemble Wraps: Place shrimp on lettuce leaves and top with avocado, tomatoes, onion, and cilantro.
4. Serve: Garnish with lime wedges if desired.

*Nutritional Information (Per Serving):  Calories: 210  Protein: 20g  Carbs: 5g  Fats: 13g  Fiber: 3g*
*Cholesterol: 150mg  Sodium: 600mg  Potassium: 450mg*

---

# Keto Bacon and Cauliflower Chowder

**Prep Time: 10 minutes**     **Cook Time: 25 minutes**     **Servings: 4**

## INGREDIENTS

- 6 slices bacon, chopped
- 1 medium head cauliflower, chopped into florets
- 1 small onion, finely chopped
- 2 cloves garlic, minced
- 4 cups chicken broth
- 1 cup heavy cream
- 1 cup shredded cheddar cheese
- 1/4 cup butter
- 1 tsp dried thyme
- Salt and pepper to taste
- Optional garnish: chopped green onions, extra shredded cheese

## COOKING PROCESS

1. Cook Bacon: In a pot, cook bacon until crispy. Remove and set aside.
2. Sauté Aromatics: Add butter to bacon fat. Sauté onion and garlic until soft.
3. Cook Cauliflower: Add cauliflower and thyme, cook 5 minutes.
4. Simmer: Add broth, simmer until cauliflower is tender.
5. Blend: Puree the soup until smooth.
6. Add Cream and Cheese: Stir in cream, cheese, and bacon. Heat through.

*Nutritional Information (Per Serving): Calories: 420  Protein: 15g  Carbs: 8g  Fats: 37g  Fiber: 3g*
*Cholesterol: 90mg  Sodium: 900mg  Potassium: 600mg*

# Cauliflower and Cheese Soup

**Prep Time: 10 minutes**     **Cook Time: 20 minutes**     **Servings: 4**

## INGREDIENTS

- 1 head cauliflower, chopped
- 1 small onion, diced
- 2 cloves garlic, minced
- 4 cups chicken or vegetable broth
- 1 cup heavy cream
- 2 cups shredded cheddar cheese
- 1/2 cup grated Parmesan cheese
- 2 tbsp butter
- Salt and pepper to taste
- Optional: chopped chives or green onions for garnish

## COOKING PROCESS

1. Cook Vegetables: In a large pot, melt butter over medium heat. Add onion and garlic, cooking until softened. Add cauliflower and broth. Bring to a boil, then reduce heat and simmer until cauliflower is tender, about 15 minutes.
2. Blend Soup: Puree the soup with an immersion blender or in batches using a regular blender until smooth.
3. Add Cream and Cheese: Stir in heavy cream, cheddar cheese, and Parmesan cheese. Cook over low heat until the cheese is melted and the soup is heated through. Season with salt and pepper to taste.
4. Serve: Ladle into bowls and garnish with chopped chives or green onions if desired.

*Nutritional Information (Per Serving): Calories: 350  Protein: 15g  Carbs: 10g  Fats: 30g  Fiber: 3g*
*Cholesterol: 90mg  Sodium: 700mg  Potassium: 400mg*

---

# Keto Clam Chowder

**Prep Time: 10 minutes**     **Cook Time: 20 minutes**     **Servings: 4**

## INGREDIENTS

- 2 tbsp butter
- 1 small onion, diced
- 2 cloves garlic, minced
- 1 cup celery, diced
- 1 cup cauliflower, finely chopped
- 2 cups clam juice
- 1 cup heavy cream
- 2 cans (6.5 oz each) chopped clams, drained
- 1/2 tsp dried thyme
- 1/2 tsp dried dill
- Salt and pepper to taste
- Optional: chopped fresh parsley for garnish

## COOKING PROCESS

1. Cook Vegetables: In a large pot, melt butter over medium heat. Add onion, garlic, and celery, cooking until softened.
2. Add Cauliflower and Clam Juice: Add cauliflower and clam juice to the pot. Bring to a boil, then reduce heat and simmer until cauliflower is tender, about 10 minutes.
3. Add Cream and Clams: Stir in heavy cream, chopped clams, thyme, and dill. Cook over low heat until heated through. Season with salt and pepper to taste.
4. Serve: Ladle into bowls and garnish with chopped fresh parsley if desired.

*Nutritional Information (Per Serving): Calories: 300  Protein: 15g  Carbs: 6g  Fats: 25g  Fiber: 2g*
*Cholesterol: 90mg  Sodium: 900mg  Potassium: 400mg*

# Creamy Asparagus Soup
**Prep Time: 10 minutes**    **Cook Time: 20 minutes**    **Servings: 4**

## INGREDIENTS

- 2 tbsp butter
- 1 small onion, diced
- 2 cloves garlic, minced
- 1 lb asparagus, trimmed and cut into 1-inch pieces
- 4 cups chicken or vegetable broth
- 1/2 cup heavy cream
- Salt and pepper to taste
- Optional: grated Parmesan cheese for garnish

## COOKING PROCESS

1. Cook Vegetables: In a large pot, melt butter over medium heat. Add onion and garlic, cooking until softened. Add asparagus and cook for 5 minutes.
2. Add Broth: Pour in the broth and bring to a boil. Reduce heat and simmer until asparagus is tender, about 10-15 minutes.
3. Blend Soup: Using an immersion blender or regular blender, puree the soup until smooth.
4. Add Cream: Stir in heavy cream and cook over low heat until heated through. Season with salt and pepper to taste.
5. Serve: Ladle into bowls and garnish with grated Parmesan cheese if desired.

*Nutritional Information (Per Serving): Calories: 200 Protein: 4g Carbs: 8g Fats: 18g Fiber: 3g*
*Cholesterol: 50mg Sodium: 600mg Potassium: 300mg*

---

# Zucchini and Parmesan Soup
**Prep Time: 10 minutes**    **Cook Time: 20 minutes**    **Servings: 4**

## INGREDIENTS

- 2 tbsp olive oil
- 1 small onion, diced
- 2 cloves garlic, minced
- 4 medium zucchinis, sliced
- 4 cups chicken or vegetable broth
- 1/2 cup grated Parmesan cheese
- 1/2 cup heavy cream
- Salt and pepper to taste
- Optional: chopped fresh basil for garnish

## COOKING PROCESS

1. Cook Vegetables: In a large pot, heat olive oil over medium heat. Add onion and garlic, cooking until softened. Add sliced zucchini and cook for 5 minutes.
2. Add Broth: Pour in the broth and bring to a boil. Reduce heat and simmer until zucchini is tender, about 10-15 minutes.
3. Blend Soup: Using an immersion blender or regular blender, puree the soup until smooth.
4. Add Cheese and Cream: Stir in grated Parmesan cheese and heavy cream. Cook over low heat until heated through. Season with salt and pepper to taste.
5. Serve: Ladle into bowls and garnish with chopped fresh basil if desired.

*Nutritional Information (Per Serving): Calories: 220 Protein: 7g Carbs: 10g Fats: 18g Fiber: 3g*
*Cholesterol: 40mg Sodium: 600mg Potassium: 400mg*

# Spicy Shrimp Keto Lettuce Wraps

**Prep Time: 10 minutes    Cook Time: 10 minutes    Servings: 4**

## INGREDIENTS

- 4 cups diced tomatoes (canned or fresh)
- 1 cup heavy cream
- 2 cups chicken broth
- 1/4 cup butter
- 1 small onion, finely chopped
- 2 cloves garlic, minced
- 1/4 cup fresh basil, chopped (or 1 tbsp dried basil)
- Salt and pepper to taste
- Optional garnish: extra chopped basil, grated Parmesan cheese

## COOKING PROCESS

1. Saute Aromatics: In a large pot, melt butter over medium heat. Add onion and garlic, saute until softened (about 3-4 minutes).

2. Add Tomatoes and Broth: Add diced tomatoes and chicken broth. Bring to a simmer and cook for 10 minutes.

3. Blend: Use an immersion blender to puree the soup until smooth, or blend in batches in a regular blender.

4. Add Cream and Basil: Stir in the heavy cream and chopped basil. Simmer for another 5 minutes. Season with salt and pepper to taste.

5. Serve: Ladle into bowls. Garnish with extra basil and grated Parmesan cheese if desired.

*Nutritional Information (Per Serving): Calories: 280  Protein: 4g  Carbs: 8g  Fats: 25g  Fiber: 2g*
*Cholesterol: 75mg  Sodium: 700mg  Potassium: 500mg*

---

# Asian Beef Keto Lettuce Wraps

**Prep Time: 10 minutes    Cook Time: 25 minutes    Servings: 4**

## INGREDIENTS

- 1 lb ground beef
- 1 tbsp olive oil
- 2 cloves garlic, minced
- 1 tbsp ginger, minced
- 2 tbsp soy sauce (or tamari for gluten-free)
- 1 tbsp rice vinegar
- 1 tbsp sesame oil
- 1 tsp chili paste (optional for heat)
- 8 large lettuce leaves
- 1/2 cup shredded carrots
- 1/2 cup sliced cucumber
- 1/4 cup green onions, chopped
- 1/4 cup fresh cilantro, chopped
- Optional: sesame seeds for garnish

## COOKING PROCESS

1. Cook Beef: Heat olive oil in a skillet over medium-high heat. Add ground beef, garlic, and ginger. Cook until beef is browned and crumbled.

2. Add Sauce: Stir in soy sauce, rice vinegar, sesame oil, and chili paste. Cook for 2-3 minutes until sauce is absorbed.

3. Assemble Wraps: Place beef mixture on lettuce leaves. Top with shredded carrots, cucumber, green onions, and cilantro.

4. Serve: Garnish with sesame seeds if desired.

*Nutritional Information (Per Serving): Calories: 250  Protein: 18g  Carbs: 6g  Fats: 18g  Fiber: 2g  Cholesterol: 70mg  Sodium: 650mg  Potassium: 400mg*

# Chicken Avocado Keto Lettuce Wraps

**Prep Time: 10 minutes     Cook Time: 10 minutes     Servings: 4**

## INGREDIENTS

- 1 lb cooked chicken breast, shredded or diced
- 1 avocado, diced
- 1/4 cup mayonnaise
- 1 tbsp lime juice
- 1 clove garlic, minced
- Salt and pepper to taste
- 8 large lettuce leaves
- 1/2 cup cherry tomatoes, halved
- 1/4 cup red onion, finely chopped
- 1/4 cup fresh cilantro, chopped
- Optional: lime wedges for serving

## COOKING PROCESS

1. Prepare Filling: In a bowl, mix shredded chicken, avocado, mayonnaise, lime juice, garlic, salt, and pepper.
2. Assemble Wraps: Place chicken avocado mixture on lettuce leaves. Top with cherry tomatoes, red onion, and cilantro.
3. Serve: Garnish with lime wedges if desired.

*Nutritional Information (Per Serving): Calories: 280  Protein: 20g  Carbs: 6g  Fats: 20g  Fiber: 4g*
*Cholesterol: 50mg  Sodium: 400mg  Potassium: 550mg*

---

# Turkey and Cheese Keto Lettuce Wraps

**Prep Time: 10 minutes     Cook Time: 0     Servings: 4**

## INGREDIENTS

- 1 lb sliced turkey breast
- 8 slices cheddar cheese (or your favorite cheese)
- 8 large lettuce leaves
- 1 avocado, sliced
- 1/2 cup cherry tomatoes, halved
- 1/4 cup red onion, thinly sliced
- 1/4 cup mayonnaise
- 1 tbsp Dijon mustard
- Salt and pepper to taste
- Optional: pickles or jalapeños for added flavor

## COOKING PROCESS

1. Prepare Dressing: In a small bowl, mix mayonnaise, Dijon mustard, salt, and pepper.
2. Assemble Wraps: Lay out lettuce leaves. Spread a thin layer of the mayonnaise mixture on each leaf.
3. Layer Ingredients: Place turkey slices, cheese, avocado, cherry tomatoes, and red onion on each leaf.
4. Roll Up: Carefully roll up the lettuce leaves to form wraps. Secure with toothpicks if needed.
5. Serve: Enjoy immediately, with pickles or jalapeños on the side if desired.

*Nutritional Information (Per Serving): Calories: 280  Protein: 25g  Carbs: 5g  Fats: 18g  Fiber: 3g  Cholesterol: 60mg  Sodium: 600mg  Potassium: 500mg*

# Almond Flour Keto Bread Loaf

**Prep Time: 10 minutes          Cook Time: 45 minutes          Servings: 1 loaf**

## INGREDIENTS

- 2 cups almond flour
- 1/4 cup coconut flour
- 1/4 cup flaxseed meal
- 1 tbsp baking powder
- 1/2 tsp salt
- 1/4 cup melted butter or coconut oil
- 6 large eggs
- 1/2 cup unsweetened almond milk
- 1 tsp apple cider vinegar

## COOKING PROCESS

1. Preheat Oven: Preheat to 350°F (175°C). Grease or line a loaf pan.
2. Mix Ingredients: Combine all dry ingredients in one bowl. In another bowl, beat eggs and add wet ingredients. Mix wet and dry together to form batter.
3. Bake: Pour batter into pan, smooth the top. Bake for 40-45 minutes until a toothpick comes out clean.
4. Cool: Cool in the pan for 10 minutes, then transfer to a wire rack.

*Nutritional Information (Per Serving): Calories: 170  Protein: 6g  Carbs: 4g  Fats: 14g  Fiber: 3g*
*Cholesterol: 70mg  Sodium: 200mg  Potassium: 80mg*

---

# Cheesy Garlic Keto Breadsticks

**Prep Time: 10 minutes          Cook Time: 20 minutes          Servings: 8 breadsticks**

## INGREDIENTS

- 2 cups shredded mozzarella cheese
- 1 cup almond flour
- 1/4 cup grated Parmesan cheese
- 1 large egg
- 2 cloves garlic, minced
- 1 tsp Italian seasoning
- 1/2 tsp baking powder
- 1/4 tsp salt
- 2 tbsp butter, melted
- Optional: fresh parsley, chopped

## COOKING PROCESS

1. Preheat Oven: Preheat to 375°F (190°C). Line a baking sheet with parchment paper.
2. Melt Cheese: Melt mozzarella in the microwave for 1-2 minutes.
3. Mix Dough: Combine all ingredients except butter. Mix in melted cheese until dough forms.
4. Shape and Bake: Shape dough into a rectangle on the baking sheet. Score into 8 breadsticks. Bake for 15-18 minutes.
5. Add Garlic Butter: Brush with melted butter. Garnish with parsley if desired.

*Nutritional Information (Per Serving): Calories: 160  Protein: 10g  Carbs: 3g  Fats: 13g  Fiber: 1g*
*Cholesterol: 35mg  Sodium: 300mg  Potassium: 50mg*

# Fluffy Coconut Flour Keto Biscuits

**Prep Time: 10 minutes     Cook Time: 20 minutes     Servings: 8 biscuits**

## INGREDIENTS

- 1/2 cup coconut flour
- 1/4 cup melted butter or coconut oil
- 4 large eggs
- 1/2 cup sour cream
- 1 tsp baking powder
- 1/2 tsp salt
- 1/4 tsp garlic powder (optional)
- 1/4 tsp onion powder (optional)

## COOKING PROCESS

1. Preheat Oven: Preheat to 375°F (190°C). Line a baking sheet with parchment paper.
2. Mix Wet Ingredients: In a bowl, whisk together melted butter, eggs, and sour cream.
3. Combine Dry Ingredients: In another bowl, mix coconut flour, baking powder, salt, garlic powder, and onion powder.
4. Form Dough: Add dry ingredients to the wet ingredients and mix until a dough forms.
5. Shape Biscuits: Scoop dough onto the prepared baking sheet, forming 8 biscuits.
6. Bake: Bake for 18-20 minutes until golden brown.

*Nutritional Information (Per Serving): Calories: 110  Protein: 4g  Carbs: 5g  Fats: 9g  Fiber: 3g*
*Cholesterol: 70mg  Sodium: 200mg  Potassium: 50mg*

---

# Herbed Keto Flatbread

**Prep Time: 10 minutes     Cook Time: 15 minutes     Servings: 4 flatbreads**

## INGREDIENTS

- 1 1/2 cups almond flour
- 1/4 cup coconut flour
- 1/4 cup flaxseed meal
- 1 tsp baking powder
- 1 tsp salt
- 1/2 tsp garlic powder
- 1/2 tsp dried oregano
- 1/2 tsp dried basil
- 1/2 cup warm water
- 1/4 cup olive oil
- 2 large eggs

## COOKING PROCESS

1. Preheat Oven: Preheat to 375°F (190°C). Line a baking sheet with parchment paper.
2. Mix Dry Ingredients: In a bowl, combine almond flour, coconut flour, flaxseed meal, baking powder, salt, garlic powder, oregano, and basil.
3. Add Wet Ingredients: Stir in warm water, olive oil, and eggs until a dough forms.
4. Shape Flatbreads: Divide dough into 4 portions. Flatten each portion into a thin round on the prepared baking sheet.
5. Bake: Bake for 12-15 minutes until golden brown.

*Nutritional Information (Per Serving): Calories: 230  Protein: 8g  Carbs: 6g  Fats: 19g  Fiber: 4g*
*Cholesterol: 55mg  Sodium: 300mg  Potassium: 70mg*

# Keto Beef Burrito Bowl

**Prep Time: 10 minutes**     **Cook Time: 20 minutes**     **Servings: 8 biscuits**

## INGREDIENTS

- 1 lb ground beef
- 1 tbsp olive oil
- 1 small onion, chopped
- 2 cloves garlic, minced
- 1 tbsp chili powder
- 1 tsp cumin
- 1/2 tsp paprika
- 1/2 tsp salt
- 1/4 tsp black pepper
- 2 cups cauliflower rice
- 1 avocado, diced
- 1/2 cup cherry tomatoes, halved
- 1/4 cup shredded cheddar cheese
- 1/4 cup sour cream
- 1/4 cup fresh cilantro, chopped
- Optional: lime wedges

## COOKING PROCESS

1. Cook Beef: Sauté onion and garlic in olive oil until soft. Add beef and cook until browned. Drain fat. Stir in spices and cook 2-3 minutes.
2. Prepare Cauliflower Rice: Cook cauliflower rice in a separate skillet until tender.
3. Assemble Bowls: Divide cauliflower rice into 4 bowls. Top with beef, avocado, tomatoes, cheese, sour cream, and cilantro.
4. Serve: Garnish with lime wedges if desired.

*Nutritional Information (Per Serving): Calories: 380  Protein: 20g  Carbs: 8g  Fats: 30g  Fiber: 4g*
*Cholesterol: 90mg  Sodium: 450mg  Potassium: 600mg*

---

# Grilled Salmon and Avocado Keto Bowl

**Prep Time: 10 minutes**     **Cook Time: 15 minutes**     **Servings: 4**

## INGREDIENTS

- 4 salmon fillets (4-6 oz each)
- 2 tbsp olive oil
- 1 tsp garlic powder
- 1 tsp paprika
- Salt and pepper to taste
- 2 cups mixed greens
- 1 avocado, diced
- 1/2 cup cherry tomatoes, halved
- 1/4 cup red onion, thinly sliced
- 1/4 cup cucumber, sliced
- 1 lemon, cut into wedges
- Optional: fresh dill for garnish

## COOKING PROCESS

1. Preheat Grill: Preheat grill to medium-high heat.
2. Season Salmon: Brush salmon fillets with olive oil. Season with garlic powder, paprika, salt, and pepper.
3. Grill Salmon: Grill salmon for 4-5 minutes per side, or until cooked to your liking. Remove from grill and let rest.
4. Assemble Bowls: Divide mixed greens among 4 bowls. Top with grilled salmon, avocado, cherry tomatoes, red onion, and cucumber.
5. Serve: Garnish with lemon wedges and fresh dill if desired.

*Nutritional Information (Per Serving): Calories: 400  Protein: 25g  Carbs: 6g  Fats: 30g  Fiber: 4g  Cholesterol: 70mg  Sodium: 300mg  Potassium: 800mg*

# Keto Chicken Pesto Zoodle Bowl

**Prep Time: 10 minutes****Cook Time: 15 minutes****Servings: 4**

## INGREDIENTS

- 2 large zucchinis, spiralized into zoodles
- 1 lb cooked chicken breast, sliced
- 1/2 cup pesto sauce (store-bought or homemade)
- 1/4 cup grated Parmesan cheese
- 1/2 cup cherry tomatoes, halved
- 1/4 cup pine nuts, toasted
- 1 tbsp olive oil
- Salt and pepper to taste
- Optional: fresh basil leaves for garnish

## COOKING PROCESS

1. Prepare Zoodles: Spiralize zucchinis to create zoodles.
2. Cook Zoodles: In a large skillet, heat olive oil over medium heat. Add zoodles and sauté for 2-3 minutes until slightly tender.
3. Add Chicken and Pesto: Add cooked chicken and pesto sauce to the skillet. Toss to combine and heat through.
4. Assemble Bowls: Divide the zoodle mixture among 4 bowls. Top with cherry tomatoes, grated Parmesan, and toasted pine nuts.
5. Serve: Garnish with fresh basil leaves if desired.

*Nutritional Information (Per Serving): Calories: 350  Protein: 30g  Carbs: 8g  Fats: 22g*
*Fiber: 3g  Cholesterol: 70mg  Sodium: 400mg  Potassium: 700mg*

---

# Pork and Cauliflower Rice Keto Bowl

**Prep Time: 10 minutes****Cook Time: 20 minutes****Servings: 4**

## INGREDIENTS

- 1 lb ground pork
- 2 tbsp olive oil
- 1 small onion, chopped
- 2 cloves garlic, minced
- 1 red bell pepper, chopped
- 1 tsp cumin
- 1 tsp smoked paprika
- 1/2 tsp salt
- 1/4 tsp black pepper
- 4 cups cauliflower rice
- 1 avocado, sliced
- 1/2 cup cherry tomatoes, halved
- 1/4 cup fresh cilantro, chopped
- Optional: lime wedges

## COOKING PROCESS

1. Cook Pork: Sauté onion and garlic in olive oil until soft. Add pork, cook until browned, and drain fat.
2. Add Spices and Veggies: Add bell pepper, cumin, paprika, salt, and pepper. Cook for 5 minutes.
3. Prepare Cauliflower Rice: Cook cauliflower rice in a separate skillet until tender.
4. Assemble Bowls: Divide cauliflower rice into 4 bowls. Top with pork, avocado, tomatoes, and cilantro.
5. Serve: Garnish with lime wedges if desired.

*Nutritional Information (Per Serving): Calories: 370  Protein: 20g  Carbs: 9g  Fats: 28g  Fiber: 4g  Cholesterol: 60mg  Sodium: 450mg  Potassium: 700mg*

# Steak and Avocado Protein Bowl

**Prep Time: 10 minutes     Cook Time: 10 minutes     Servings: 4**

## INGREDIENTS

- 8 oz steak, cooked and sliced
- 1 avocado, sliced
- 2 cups mixed greens
- 1/2 cup cherry tomatoes, halved
- 1/4 cup red onion, sliced
- 1/4 cup crumbled feta cheese
- 2 tbsp olive oil
- 1 tbsp balsamic vinegar
- Salt and pepper to taste

## COOKING PROCESS

1. Prepare Steak: Season the steak with salt and pepper. Cook to desired doneness in a skillet over medium-high heat. Let rest, then slice.
2. Assemble Bowl: In two bowls, divide the mixed greens, cherry tomatoes, red onion, and feta cheese.
3. Add Steak and Avocado: Top each bowl with sliced steak and avocado.
4. Dress: Drizzle with olive oil and balsamic vinegar. Season with salt and pepper to taste.
5. Serve: Serve immediately.

*Nutritional Information (Per Serving): Calories: 450  Protein: 25g  Carbs: 10g  Fats: 35g  Fiber: 7g*
*Cholesterol: 60mg  Sodium: 300mg  Potassium: 900mg*

---

# Keto Beef Bulgogi Bowl

**Prep Time: 10 minutes     Cook Time: 10 minutes     Servings: 4**

## INGREDIENTS

- 8 oz beef sirloin, thinly sliced
- 2 tbsp soy sauce (or tamari)
- 1 tbsp sesame oil
- 1 tbsp erythritol
- 2 cloves garlic, minced
- 1 tsp grated ginger
- 1/2 small onion, sliced
- 2 cups cauliflower rice
- 1 cup spinach
- 1/2 avocado, sliced
- 1 green onion, chopped
- 1 tsp sesame seeds

## COOKING PROCESS

1. Marinate Beef: Mix soy sauce, sesame oil, erythritol, garlic, and ginger. Add beef and marinate for 10 minutes.
2. Cook Beef: Sauté beef and onions until cooked.
3. Cook Cauliflower Rice: Sauté cauliflower rice until tender. Add spinach and cook until wilted.
4. Assemble Bowls: Divide cauliflower rice, spinach, beef, and onions between two bowls.
5. Add Toppings: Top with avocado, green onion, and sesame seeds.

*Nutritional Information (Per Serving): Calories: 350  Protein: 25g  Carbs: 8g  Fats: 25g  Fiber: 4g*
*Cholesterol: 70mg  Sodium: 800mg  Potassium: 700mg*

# Turkey and Spinach Power Bowl

**Prep Time: 10 minutes**     **Cook Time: 10 minutes**     **Servings: 2**

## INGREDIENTS

- 8 oz ground turkey
- 2 cups fresh spinach
- 1/2 cup cherry tomatoes, halved
- 1/2 avocado, sliced
- 1/4 cup red onion, thinly sliced
- 2 tbsp olive oil
- 1 tbsp balsamic vinegar
- Salt and pepper to taste
- Optional: feta cheese for garnish

## COOKING PROCESS

1. Cook Turkey: In a skillet, cook ground turkey over medium heat until fully cooked. Season with salt and pepper.
2. Wilt Spinach: Add fresh spinach to the skillet and cook until wilted.
3. Assemble Bowls: Divide the turkey and spinach mixture between two bowls. Add cherry tomatoes, avocado slices, and red onion.
4. Dress: Drizzle with olive oil and balsamic vinegar. Season with salt and pepper.
5. Serve: Garnish with feta cheese if desired. Serve immediately.

*Nutritional Information (Per Serving): Calories: 300  Protein: 25g  Carbs: 8g  Fats: 20g  Fiber: 4g*
*Cholesterol: 70mg  Sodium: 400mg  Potassium: 700mg*

---

# Tuna Poke Keto Bowl

**Prep Time: 15 minutes**     **Cook Time: 0 minutes**     **Servings: 2**

## INGREDIENTS

- 8 oz sashimi-grade tuna, cubed
- 2 tbsp soy sauce (or tamari)
- 1 tbsp sesame oil
- 1 tsp rice vinegar
- 1 avocado, cubed
- 1 cucumber, sliced
- 1/4 cup red cabbage, sliced
- 2 tbsp green onions, chopped
- 1 tbsp sesame seeds
- 1/2 cup cauliflower rice, cooked and cooled

## COOKING PROCESS

1. Marinate Tuna: Combine soy sauce, sesame oil, and rice vinegar. Add tuna and marinate for 10 minutes.
2. Prepare Bowl: Divide cauliflower rice between two bowls. Arrange avocado, cucumber, and red cabbage.
3. Add Tuna: Top with marinated tuna and remaining marinade.
4. Garnish: Sprinkle with green onions and sesame seeds. Serve immediately.

*Nutritional Information (Per Serving): Calories: 350  Protein: 25g  Carbs: 10g  Fats: 25g  Fiber: 7g*
*Cholesterol: 45mg  Sodium: 600mg  Potassium: 800mg*

# Cilantro Lime Cauliflower Rice

**Prep Time: 5 minutes**     **Cook Time: 10 minutes**     **Servings: 4**

Creative Ways to Use Cauliflower Rice

## INGREDIENTS

- 4 cups cauliflower rice
- 2 tbsp olive oil
- 2 cloves garlic, minced
- 1/4 cup fresh cilantro, chopped
- Juice of 1 lime
- Salt and pepper to taste

## COOKING PROCESS

1. Cook Garlic: Heat olive oil in a large skillet over medium heat. Add minced garlic and sauté for 1-2 minutes until fragrant.
2. Cook Cauliflower Rice: Add cauliflower rice to the skillet. Cook, stirring occasionally, until tender (about 5-7 minutes).
3. Add Cilantro and Lime: Remove from heat. Stir in fresh cilantro and lime juice. Season with salt and pepper to taste.
4. Serve: Transfer to a serving dish and enjoy.

*Nutritional Information (Per Serving): Calories: 70 Protein: 2g Carbs: 5g Fats: 5g Fiber: 2g*
*Cholesterol: 0mg Sodium: 60mg Potassium: 200mg*

---

# Keto Cauliflower Fried Rice

**Prep Time: 10 minutes**     **Cook Time: 15 minutes**     **Servings: 4**

## INGREDIENTS

- 4 cups cauliflower rice
- 2 tbsp olive oil
- 1 small onion, chopped
- 2 cloves garlic, minced
- 1 cup mixed vegetables

(e.g., peas, carrots, bell peppers), chopped

- 2 large eggs, beaten
- 3 tbsp soy sauce (or tamari for gluten-free)
- 1 tbsp sesame oil
- 1/4 cup green onions, sliced
- Salt and pepper to taste

## COOKING PROCESS

1. Cook Onion and Garlic: Heat olive oil in a large skillet over medium heat. Add chopped onion and garlic, sauté until softened (about 3-4 minutes).
2. Add Vegetables: Add mixed vegetables and cook for 3-4 minutes until tender.
3. Cook Cauliflower Rice: Add cauliflower rice to the skillet and cook for 5-7 minutes, stirring occasionally, until tender.
4. Scramble Eggs: Push the cauliflower rice mixture to one side of the skillet. Pour beaten eggs into the other side and scramble until fully cooked.
5. Combine and Season: Stir everything together. Add soy sauce, sesame oil, salt, and pepper. Cook for an additional 2 minutes.
6. Serve: Garnish with sliced green onions and serve hot.

*Nutritional Information (Per Serving): Calories: 150 Protein: 6g Carbs: 8g Fats: 11g Fiber: 3g Cholesterol: 70mg Sodium: 600mg Potassium: 300mg*

# Cauliflower Rice Risotto with Mushrooms

**Prep Time: 10 minutes          Cook Time: 20 minutes          Servings: 4**

## INGREDIENTS

- 4 cups cauliflower rice
- 2 tbsp olive oil
- 1 small onion, finely chopped
- 2 cloves garlic, minced
- 2 cups mushrooms, sliced
- 1/2 cup heavy cream
- 1/2 cup grated Parmesan cheese
- 1/4 cup chicken or vegetable broth
- 1/4 cup dry white wine (optional)
- 1 tbsp fresh parsley, chopped
- Salt and pepper to taste

## COOKING PROCESS

1. Cook Onion and Garlic: Heat olive oil in a large skillet over medium heat. Add chopped onion and garlic, sauté until softened (about 3-4 minutes).
2. Cook Mushrooms: Add sliced mushrooms to the skillet and cook until tender and browned (about 5-7 minutes).
3. Add Cauliflower Rice: Stir in the cauliflower rice and cook for 5 minutes, stirring occasionally.
4. Add Liquid: Add heavy cream, Parmesan cheese, broth, and white wine (if using). Cook for another 5 minutes until the mixture is creamy and the cauliflower rice is tender.
5. Season and Serve: Stir in fresh parsley. Season with salt and pepper to taste. Serve hot.

*Nutritional Information (Per Serving): Calories: 220  Protein: 8g  Carbs: 8g  Fats: 18g  Fiber: 3g  Cholesterol: 50mg  Sodium: 400mg  Potassium: 400mg*

# Cauliflower Rice and Spinach Stuffed Peppers

**Prep Time: 15 minutes          Cook Time: 30 minutes          Servings: 4**

## INGREDIENTS

- 4 large bell peppers, tops cut off and seeds removed
- 2 cups cauliflower rice
- 2 tbsp olive oil
- 1 small onion, chopped
- 2 cloves garlic, minced
- 2 cups fresh spinach, chopped
- 1/2 cup sugar-free marinara sauce
- 1/2 cup shredded mozzarella cheese
- 1/4 cup grated Parmesan cheese
- Salt and pepper to taste
- Optional: fresh basil or parsley for garnish

## COOKING PROCESS

1. Preheat Oven: Preheat to 375°F (190°C).
2. Cook Filling: Sauté onion and garlic in olive oil until soft. Add cauliflower rice and spinach, cook until tender.
3. Mix: Stir in marinara sauce, half the mozzarella, and Parmesan. Season with salt and pepper.
4. Stuff Peppers: Fill peppers with mixture, place in baking dish. Top with remaining mozzarella.
5. Bake: Bake for 25-30 minutes until peppers are tender and cheese is melted.
6. Serve: Garnish with fresh basil or parsley if desired.

*Nutritional Information (Per Serving): Calories: 200  Protein: 8g  Carbs: 10g  Fats: 14g  Fiber: 3g  Cholesterol: 20mg  Sodium: 400mg  Potassium: 600mg*

# CHAPTER 4: DINNER RECIPES

# Garlic Butter Chicken Thighs with Asparagus

**Prep Time: 10 minutes     Cook Time: 25 minutes     Servings: 4**

## INGREDIENTS

- 1 1/2 lbs chicken thighs (bone-in, skin-on)
- 2 tbsp olive oil
- 4 cloves garlic, minced
- 1 lb asparagus, trimmed
- 1/4 cup butter
- 1 tbsp lemon juice
- Salt and pepper to taste
- Optional: lemon wedges

## COOKING PROCESS

1. Preheat Oven: Preheat to 400°F (200°C).
2. Sear Chicken: Season chicken with salt and pepper. Sear in olive oil, skin-side down, until golden (5-7 minutes). Flip and cook 3-4 minutes. Remove chicken.
3. Cook Asparagus: Add garlic to the skillet, cook 1 minute. Add asparagus, cook 3-4 minutes until tender.
4. Add Butter and Lemon: Stir in butter and lemon juice until melted.
5. Bake: Return chicken to skillet, skin-side up. Bake for 15-20 minutes until cooked through.
6. Serve: Garnish with lemon wedges if desired.

*Nutritional Information (Per Serving): Calories: 350  Protein: 25g  Carbs: 5g  Fats: 25g  Fiber: 2g  Cholesterol: 130mg Sodium: 250mg  Potassium: 500mg*

---

# Beef and Broccoli Stir-Fry

**Prep Time: 10 minutes     Cook Time: 15 minutes     Servings: 4**

## INGREDIENTS

- 1 lb beef sirloin, thinly sliced
- 2 tbsp olive oil
- 4 cups broccoli florets
- 1 small onion, thinly sliced
- 3 cloves garlic, minced
- 1/4 cup soy sauce (or tamari for gluten-free)
- 2 tbsp oyster sauce
- 1 tbsp sesame oil
- 1 tsp grated ginger
- 1/2 tsp red pepper flakes (optional)
- Salt and pepper to taste
- Optional: sesame seeds for garnish

## COOKING PROCESS

1. Prepare Beef: Season sliced beef with salt and pepper.
2. Cook Beef: Heat olive oil in a large skillet over medium-high heat. Cook beef until browned (about 3-4 minutes). Remove from skillet and set aside.
3. Cook Vegetables: In the same skillet, add onion and garlic. Sauté until fragrant (about 2 minutes). Add broccoli and cook until tender (about 5-7 minutes).
4. Combine: Return beef to the skillet. Stir in soy sauce, oyster sauce, sesame oil, ginger, and red pepper flakes (if using). Cook for another 2-3 minutes until everything is well coated and heated through.
5. Serve: Garnish with sesame seeds if desired.

*Nutritional Information (Per Serving): Calories: 320  Protein: 25g  Carbs: 8g  Fats: 20g  Fiber: 3g  Cholesterol: 70mg  Sodium: 800mg  Potassium: 500mg*

# Pork Chops with Creamy Mushroom Sauce

**Prep Time: 10 minutes     Cook Time: 20 minutes     Servings: 4**

## INGREDIENTS

- 4 pork chops
- 2 tbsp olive oil
- 2 cups sliced mushrooms
- 1 small onion, chopped
- 3 cloves garlic, minced
- 1/2 cup heavy cream
- 1/2 cup chicken broth
- 1 tsp Dijon mustard
- Salt and pepper to taste
- Optional: fresh parsley, chopped

## COOKING PROCESS

1. Sear Pork Chops: Season pork chops with salt and pepper. Sear in olive oil until golden (3-4 minutes per side). Remove from skillet.
2. Cook Mushrooms: In the same skillet, sauté onion and garlic for 2 minutes. Add mushrooms and cook until tender (5 minutes).
3. Make Sauce: Add chicken broth, cream, and Dijon mustard. Simmer until thickened (5 minutes).
4. Combine: Return pork chops to skillet, spoon sauce over, and cook for 3-4 minutes.
5. Serve: Garnish with fresh parsley if desired.

*Nutritional Information (Per Serving): Calories: 400  Protein: 28g  Carbs: 6g  Fats: 28g  Fiber: 1g  Cholesterol: 120mg Sodium: 350mg  Potassium: 700mg*

---

# Herb-Crusted Lamb Chops

**Prep Time: 10 minutes     Cook Time: 15 minutes     Servings: 4**

## INGREDIENTS

- 8 lamb chops
- 2 tbsp olive oil
- 1/4 cup fresh parsley, chopped
- 1/4 cup fresh rosemary, chopped
- 1/4 cup fresh thyme, chopped
- 3 cloves garlic, minced
- Salt and pepper to taste
- Optional: lemon wedges for serving

## COOKING PROCESS

1. Preheat Oven: Preheat to 400°F (200°C).
2. Prepare Herb Mixture: In a bowl, mix parsley, rosemary, thyme, garlic, salt, and pepper.
3. Coat Lamb Chops: Brush lamb chops with olive oil. Press herb mixture onto both sides of the chops.
4. Sear Lamb Chops: Heat a skillet over medium-high heat. Sear lamb chops for 2-3 minutes per side until browned.
5. Bake: Transfer lamb chops to a baking sheet. Bake for 5-7 minutes until desired doneness.
6. Serve: Garnish with lemon wedges if desired.

*Nutritional Information (Per Serving): Calories: 320  Protein: 24g  Carbs: 2g  Fats: 24g  Fiber: 1g Cholesterol: 80mg  Sodium: 300mg  Potassium: 400mg*

# Keto BBQ Pork Ribs with Coleslaw

**Prep Time: 15 minutes   Cook Time: 2.5 hours   Servings: 4**

## INGREDIENTS

BBQ Pork Ribs:
- 2 lbs pork ribs
- 1 tbsp olive oil
- 1 tbsp smoked paprika
- 1 tsp garlic powder
- 1 tsp onion powder
- 1 tsp salt
- 1/2 tsp black pepper
- 1/2 cup sugar-free BBQ sauce

Coleslaw:
- 2 cups shredded cabbage
- 1 cup shredded carrots
- 1/4 cup mayonnaise
- 1 tbsp apple cider vinegar
- 1 tbsp erythritol
- Salt and pepper to taste

## COOKING PROCESS

1. Preheat Oven: Preheat to 300°F (150°C).
2. Prepare Ribs: Rub ribs with olive oil and spices. Wrap in foil.
3. Bake Ribs: Bake wrapped ribs for 2 hours. Unwrap, brush with BBQ sauce, and bake uncovered for 30 minutes.
4. Prepare Coleslaw: Mix cabbage, carrots, mayonnaise, apple cider vinegar, erythritol, salt, and pepper.
5. Serve: Serve ribs with coleslaw.

*Nutritional Information (Per Serving): BBQ Pork Ribs:  Calories: 400 Protein: 30g  Carbs: 3g  Fats: 30g  Fiber: 1g  Cholesterol: 100mg Sodium: 800mg  Potassium: 400mg*

*Coleslaw:  Calories: 100  Protein: 1g  Carbs: 5g  Fats: 9g  Fiber: 2g Cholesterol: 5mg  Sodium: 150mg  Potassium: 150mg*

# Beef and Vegetable Kebabs

**Prep Time: 15 minutes   Cook Time: 15 minutes   Servings: 4**

## INGREDIENTS

- 1 lb beef sirloin, cut into 1-inch cubes
- 1 red bell pepper, cut into 1-inch pieces
- 1 yellow bell pepper, cut into 1-inch pieces
- 1 zucchini, sliced into thick rounds
- 1 red onion, cut into wedges
- 1/4 cup olive oil
- 2 tbsp soy sauce (or tamari for gluten-free)
- 2 cloves garlic, minced
- 1 tsp dried oregano
- 1 tsp black pepper
- Salt to taste
- Wooden or metal skewers

## COOKING PROCESS

1. Prepare Marinade: In a bowl, mix olive oil, soy sauce, garlic, oregano, black pepper, and salt.
2. Marinate Beef: Add beef cubes to the marinade and let sit for at least 15 minutes.
3. Assemble Kebabs: Thread beef, bell peppers, zucchini, and red onion onto skewers, alternating between each ingredient.
4. Preheat Grill: Preheat grill to medium-high heat.
5. Grill Kebabs: Grill kebabs for about 10-15 minutes, turning occasionally, until beef is cooked to desired doneness and vegetables are tender.
6. Serve: Serve immediately.

*Nutritional Information (Per Serving): Calories: 300  Protein: 25g  Carbs: 8g  Fats: 18g  Fiber: 2g  Cholesterol: 70mg  Sodium: 300mg  Potassium: 600mg*

# Slow-Cooker Chicken Alfredo

**Prep Time: 10 minutes**     **Cook Time: 4-6 hours**     **Servings: 4**

## INGREDIENTS

- 4 boneless, skinless chicken breasts
- 1 cup heavy cream
- 1/2 cup chicken broth
- 4 cloves garlic, minced
- 1/2 cup grated Parmesan cheese
- 1 tsp Italian seasoning
- Salt and pepper to taste
- Optional: chopped parsley for garnish

## COOKING PROCESS

1. Prepare Chicken: Season chicken breasts with salt, pepper, and Italian seasoning. Place in slow cooker.
2. Add Ingredients: Add heavy cream, chicken broth, and minced garlic to the slow cooker.
3. Cook: Cover and cook on low for 4-6 hours or until the chicken is tender and cooked through.
4. Add Cheese: About 15 minutes before serving, stir in the Parmesan cheese until melted and the sauce is creamy.
5. Serve: Garnish with chopped parsley if desired.

*Nutritional Information (Per Serving): Calories: 400  Protein: 35g  Carbs: 2g  Fats: 28g  Fiber: 0g  Cholesterol: 140mg Sodium: 350mg  Potassium: 600mg*

---

# Instant Pot Beef Stew

**Prep Time: 10 minutes**     **Cook Time: 35 minutes**     **Servings: 6**

## INGREDIENTS

- 2 lbs beef stew meat, cubed
- 2 tbsp olive oil
- 1 onion, chopped
- 3 cloves garlic, minced
- 4 cups beef broth
- 1 cup celery, chopped
- 2 cups carrots, chopped
- 1 cup tomatoes, diced
- 1 cup turnips, diced (optional)
- 1 tbsp Worcestershire sauce
- 1 tsp dried thyme
- 1 tsp dried rosemary
- 1 tsp salt
- 1/2 tsp black pepper
- 2 tbsp tomato paste
- Optional: fresh parsley for garnish

## COOKING PROCESS

1. Saute Beef: Set Instant Pot to sauté. Heat oil, brown beef, remove.
2. Cook Aromatics: Sauté onion and garlic until soft.
3. Combine: Add beef, broth, veggies, Worcestershire, herbs, salt, pepper, tomato paste.
4. Pressure Cook: High pressure for 35 minutes. Natural release 10 minutes, then quick release.
5. Serve: Garnish with parsley if desired.

*Nutritional Information (Per Serving): Calories: 300  Protein: 25g  Carbs: 10g  Fats: 18g  Fiber: 2g Cholesterol: 80mg  Sodium: 600mg  Potassium: 700mg*

# Slow-Cooker Pulled Pork

**Prep Time: 10 minutes          Cook Time: 8 hours          Servings: 8**

## INGREDIENTS

- 4 lbs pork shoulder
- 1 large onion, sliced
- 4 cloves garlic, minced
- 1 cup chicken broth
- 1/2 cup apple cider vinegar
- 1/4 cup tomato paste
- 2 tbsp paprika
- 1 tbsp chili powder
- 1 tbsp cumin
- 1 tsp salt
- 1/2 tsp black pepper
- Optional: BBQ sauce for serving

## COOKING PROCESS

1. Prepare Pork: Season pork shoulder with paprika, chili powder, cumin, salt, and pepper.
2. Layer Ingredients: Place sliced onion and minced garlic in the slow cooker. Place pork on top.
3. Add Liquids: Mix chicken broth, apple cider vinegar, and tomato paste. Pour over pork.
4. Cook: Cover and cook on low for 8 hours or until pork is tender and easily shredded.
5. Shred and Serve: Remove pork, shred with forks, and return to the slow cooker to mix with juices. Serve with BBQ sauce if desired.

*Nutritional Information (Per Serving): Calories: 400  Protein: 30g  Carbs: 5g  Fats: 28g  Fiber: 1g  Cholesterol: 100mg Sodium: 500mg  Potassium: 600mg*

---

# Instant Pot Lamb Curry

**Prep Time: 10 minutes          Cook Time: 40 minutes          Servings: 4**

## INGREDIENTS

- 1 1/2 lbs lamb shoulder, cubed
- 2 tbsp olive oil
- 1 large onion, chopped
- 3 cloves garlic, minced
- 1 tbsp ginger, minced
- 2 tbsp curry powder
- 1 tsp ground cumin
- 1 tsp ground coriander
- 1/2 tsp turmeric
- 1/2 tsp cayenne pepper (optional)
- 1 can (14 oz) diced tomatoes
- 1 cup coconut milk
- 1/2 cup chicken broth
- Salt and pepper to taste
- Optional: fresh cilantro for garnish

## COOKING PROCESS

1. Sauté Lamb: Set Instant Pot to sauté. Heat oil, brown lamb, remove.
2. Cook Aromatics: Sauté onion, garlic, and ginger until soft. Add spices, cook 1 minute.
3. Combine Ingredients: Add lamb, tomatoes, coconut milk, and broth.
4. Pressure Cook: High pressure for 35 minutes. Natural release 10 minutes, then quick release.
5. Serve: Garnish with cilantro if desired.

*Nutritional Information (Per Serving): Calories: 450  Protein: 25g  Carbs: 10g  Fats: 35g  Fiber: 3g Cholesterol: 90mg  Sodium: 600mg  Potassium: 700mg*

# Lemon Garlic Butter Salmon

**Prep Time: 10 minutes    Cook Time: 15 minutes    Servings: 4**

## INGREDIENTS

- 4 salmon fillets (4-6 oz each)
- 2 tbsp olive oil
- 1/4 cup butter, melted
- 4 cloves garlic, minced
- Juice of 1 lemon
- Zest of 1 lemon
- Salt and pepper to taste
- Optional: fresh parsley for garnish

## COOKING PROCESS

1. Preheat Oven: Preheat to 400°F (200°C).
2. Prepare Salmon: Place salmon fillets on a baking sheet. Season with salt and pepper.
3. Make Sauce: In a bowl, mix melted butter, minced garlic, lemon juice, and lemon zest.
4. Bake: Pour sauce over salmon. Bake for 12-15 minutes until salmon is cooked through.
5. Serve: Garnish with fresh parsley if desired.

*Nutritional Information (Per Serving): Calories: 350  Protein: 25g  Carbs: 2g  Fats: 27g  Fiber: 0g  Cholesterol: 90mg Sodium: 300mg  Potassium: 600mg*

---

# Shrimp Scampi with Zoodles

**Prep Time: 10 minutes    Cook Time: 10 minutes    Servings: 4**

## INGREDIENTS

- 1 lb shrimp, peeled and deveined
- 4 zucchinis, spiralized
- 3 tbsp olive oil
- 4 cloves garlic, minced
- 1/4 cup white wine (optional)
- Juice of 1 lemon
- 1/4 cup butter
- Salt and pepper to taste
- 1/4 tsp red pepper flakes (optional)
- 1/4 cup fresh parsley, chopped
- Optional: grated Parmesan cheese

## COOKING PROCESS

1. Cook Shrimp: Heat 1 tbsp olive oil in a skillet. Cook shrimp until pink, 2-3 minutes per side. Remove.
2. Sauté Garlic: Add remaining olive oil and garlic to the skillet. Sauté 1 minute.
3. Add Wine and Lemon: Add wine (if using) and lemon juice. Cook 2-3 minutes. Stir in butter.
4. Cook Zoodles: Add zoodles, toss to coat, and cook 2-3 minutes until tender.
5. Combine: Return shrimp to skillet. Season with red pepper flakes, salt, and pepper.
6. Serve: Garnish with parsley and Parmesan if desired.

*Nutritional Information (Per Serving): Calories: 280  Protein: 20g  Carbs: 6g  Fats: 20g  Fiber: 2g Cholesterol: 180mg  Sodium: 600mg  Potassium: 500mg*

# Baked Cod with Herb Butter

**Prep Time: 10 minutes**   **Cook Time: 15 minutes**   **Servings: 4**

## INGREDIENTS

- 4 cod fillets (4-6 oz each)
- 1/4 cup butter, melted
- 2 tbsp fresh parsley, chopped
- 2 tbsp fresh dill, chopped
- 2 cloves garlic, minced
- Juice of 1 lemon
- Salt and pepper to taste
- Optional: lemon wedges for serving

## COOKING PROCESS

1. Preheat Oven: Preheat to 400°F (200°C).
2. Prepare Herb Butter: In a bowl, mix melted butter, parsley, dill, garlic, lemon juice, salt, and pepper.
3. Season Cod: Place cod fillets on a baking sheet. Brush with herb butter.
4. Bake: Bake for 12-15 minutes until cod is flaky and cooked through.
5. Serve: Garnish with lemon wedges if desired.

*Nutritional Information (Per Serving): Calories: 220  Protein: 20g  Carbs: 2g  Fats: 15g  Fiber: 0g  Cholesterol: 80mg  Sodium: 250mg  Potassium: 400mg*

---

# Grilled Tuna Steaks with Avocado Salsa

**Prep Time: 10 minutes**   **Cook Time: 10 minutes**   **Servings: 4**

## INGREDIENTS

- 4 tuna steaks (6 oz each)
- 2 tbsp olive oil
- Salt and pepper to taste
- 1 avocado, diced
- 1/2 cup cherry tomatoes, halved
- 1/4 cup red onion, finely chopped
- 1/4 cup fresh cilantro, chopped
- Juice of 1 lime
- Optional: lime wedges for serving

## COOKING PROCESS

1. Preheat Grill: Preheat grill to medium-high heat.
2. Season Tuna: Brush tuna steaks with olive oil. Season with salt and pepper.
3. Grill Tuna: Grill tuna steaks for 3-4 minutes per side, or until desired doneness.
4. Prepare Salsa: In a bowl, mix diced avocado, cherry tomatoes, red onion, cilantro, and lime juice. Season with salt and pepper.
5. Serve: Top grilled tuna steaks with avocado salsa. Garnish with lime wedges if desired.

*Nutritional Information (Per Serving): Calories: 350  Protein: 35g  Carbs: 8g  Fats: 20g  Fiber: 4g  Cholesterol: 70mg  Sodium: 250mg  Potassium: 800mg*

# Creamy Seafood Chowder

**Prep Time: 15 minutes**     **Cook Time: 25 minutes**     **Servings: 4**

## INGREDIENTS

- 1 lb mixed seafood (shrimp, scallops, white fish), bite-sized pieces
- 2 tbsp butter
- 1 onion, chopped
- 2 cloves garlic, minced
- 2 celery stalks, chopped
- 2 cups cauliflower florets, finely chopped
- 4 cups seafood or chicken broth
- 1 cup heavy cream
- 1 tsp dried thyme
- 1 tsp dried dill
- Salt and pepper to taste
- Optional: fresh parsley for garnish

## COOKING PROCESS

1. Sauté Vegetables: Melt butter in a pot over medium heat. Sauté onion, garlic, and celery until soft (5 minutes).
2. Cook Cauliflower: Add cauliflower, cook 5 minutes.
3. Simmer: Add broth, bring to a boil, then simmer for 10 minutes. Blend until smooth.
4. Add Seafood: Add seafood, cream, thyme, dill, salt, and pepper. Simmer 5-7 minutes until seafood is cooked.
5. Serve: Garnish with parsley if desired.

*Nutritional Information (Per Serving): Calories: 320  Protein: 25g  Carbs: 8g  Fats: 20g  Fiber: 2g  Cholesterol: 150mg Sodium: 600mg  Potassium: 700mg*

---

# Spicy Shrimp and Sausage Stew

**Prep Time: 10 minutes**     **Cook Time: 25 minutes**     **Servings: 4**

## INGREDIENTS

- 1 lb shrimp, peeled and deveined
- 1/2 lb smoked sausage, sliced
- 2 tbsp olive oil
- 1 onion, chopped
- 2 cloves garlic, minced
- 1 bell pepper, chopped
- 1 can (14.5 oz) diced tomatoes
- 2 cups chicken broth
- 1 tsp smoked paprika
- 1/2 tsp cayenne pepper
- 1 tsp dried thyme
- Salt and pepper to taste
- Optional: fresh parsley for garnish

## COOKING PROCESS

1. Cook Sausage: Brown sausage in olive oil, remove.
2. Sauté Vegetables: Sauté onion, garlic, and bell pepper in the same pot until soft.
3. Simmer Stew: Add tomatoes, broth, paprika, cayenne, thyme, salt, and pepper. Simmer with sausage for 10 minutes.
4. Add Shrimp: Add shrimp, cook until pink.
5. Serve: Garnish with parsley if desired.

*Nutritional Information (Per Serving): Calories: 300  Protein: 25g  Carbs: 10g  Fats: 18g  Fiber: 2g  Cholesterol: 150mg  Sodium: 800mg  Potassium: 600mg*

# Keto Clam Chowder

**Prep Time: 10 minutes    Cook Time: 20 minutes    Servings: 4**

## INGREDIENTS

- 2 cans (6.5 oz each) clams, with juice
- 4 slices bacon, chopped
- 1 small onion, chopped
- 2 cloves garlic, minced
- 2 cups cauliflower florets, finely chopped
- 2 cups chicken broth
- 1 cup heavy cream
- 1 tsp dried thyme
- Salt and pepper to taste
- Optional: fresh parsley for garnish

## COOKING PROCESS

1. Cook Bacon: In a pot, cook bacon until crispy. Remove, keep bacon fat.
2. Sauté Vegetables: Sauté onion and garlic in bacon fat until soft.
3. Cook Cauliflower: Add cauliflower, cook 5 minutes.
4. Add Liquids: Add broth, clam juice, and thyme. Simmer 10 minutes.
5. Add Clams and Cream: Stir in clams and cream, cook 5 minutes.
6. Serve: Garnish with bacon and parsley if desired.

*Nutritional Information (Per Serving): Calories: 300  Protein: 15g  Carbs: 7g  Fats: 24g  Fiber: 2g*
*Cholesterol: 80mg  Sodium: 700mg  Potassium: 500mg*

---

# Fish and Tomato Stew

**Prep Time: 10 minutes    Cook Time: 20 minutes    Servings: 4**

## INGREDIENTS

- 1 lb white fish fillets, bite-sized pieces
- 2 tbsp olive oil
- 1 onion, chopped
- 2 cloves garlic, minced
- 2 cloves garlic, minced
- 1 bell pepper, chopped
- 1 can (14.5 oz) diced tomatoes
- 2 cups fish or chicken broth
- 1 tsp dried oregano
- 1 tsp dried basil
- Salt and pepper to taste
- Optional: fresh parsley for garnish

## COOKING PROCESS

1. Sauté Vegetables: Heat oil in a pot, sauté onion, garlic, and bell pepper until soft.
2. Simmer: Add tomatoes, broth, oregano, basil, salt, and pepper. Bring to a simmer.
3. Add Fish: Add fish, simmer 10-15 minutes until cooked.
4. Serve: Garnish with parsley if desired.

*Nutritional Information (Per Serving): Calories: 200  Protein: 25g  Carbs: 8g  Fats: 8g Fiber: 2g*
*Cholesterol: 60mg  Sodium: 400mg  Potassium: 700mg*

# Spinach and Feta Stuffed Portobello Mushrooms

**Prep Time: 10 minutes    Cook Time: 20 minutes    Servings: 4**

## INGREDIENTS

- 4 large portobello mushrooms, stems removed
- 2 tbsp olive oil
- 3 cloves garlic, minced
- 4 cups fresh spinach, chopped
- 1/2 cup crumbled feta cheese
- 1/4 cup grated Parmesan cheese
- Salt and pepper to taste
- Optional: fresh parsley for garnish

## COOKING PROCESS

1. Preheat Oven: Preheat to 375°F (190°C). Brush mushrooms with olive oil and place on a baking sheet.
2. Sauté Spinach: In a skillet, heat remaining olive oil. Sauté garlic until fragrant, then add spinach and cook until wilted. Season with salt and pepper.
3. Stuff Mushrooms: Divide spinach mixture among the mushrooms. Top with crumbled feta and grated Parmesan.
4. Bake: Bake for 15-20 minutes until mushrooms are tender and cheese is melted.
5. Serve: Garnish with fresh parsley if desired.

*Nutritional Information (Per Serving): Calories: 150  Protein: 6g  Carbs: 6g  Fats: 12g  Fiber: 2g  Cholesterol: 15mg Sodium: 350mg  Potassium: 600mg*

---

# Cauliflower Mac and Cheese

**Prep Time: 10 minutes    Cook Time: 20 minutes    Servings: 4**

## INGREDIENTS

- 1 large head cauliflower, cut into florets
- 2 tbsp butter
- 1 cup heavy cream
- 1 1/2 cups shredded cheddar cheese
- 1/2 cup grated Parmesan cheese
- 1/2 tsp garlic powder
- 1/2 tsp onion powder
- Salt and pepper to tas
- Optional: chopped parsley for garnish

## COOKING PROCESS

1. Cook Cauliflower: Boil cauliflower florets until tender, about 5-7 minutes. Drain and set aside.
2. Make Cheese Sauce: In a large pot, melt butter over medium heat. Add heavy cream and bring to a simmer. Stir in cheddar cheese, Parmesan cheese, garlic powder, onion powder, salt, and pepper until smooth.
3. Combine: Add cauliflower to the cheese sauce and stir until well coated.
4. Serve: Garnish with chopped parsley if desired.

*Nutritional Information (Per Serving): Calories: 320  Protein: 15g  Carbs: 8g  Fats: 28g  Fiber: 3g Cholesterol: 90mg  Sodium: 500mg  Potassium: 600mg*

# Zucchini Noodles with Pesto

**Prep Time: 10 minutes    Cook Time: 5 minutes    Servings: 4**

## INGREDIENTS

- 4 zucchinis, spiralized into noodles
- 1/4 cup olive oil
- 1/2 cup pesto sauce (store-bought or homemade)
- 1/4 cup grated Parmesan cheese
- Salt and pepper to taste
- Optional: cherry tomatoes, halved for garnish
- Optional: pine nuts for garnish

## COOKING PROCESS

1. Cook Zucchini Noodles: Heat olive oil in a large skillet over medium heat. Add zucchini noodles and sauté for 2-3 minutes until just tender.
2. Add Pesto: Remove skillet from heat. Toss zucchini noodles with pesto sauce until evenly coated.
3. Serve: Top with grated Parmesan cheese, salt, and pepper. Garnish with cherry tomatoes and pine nuts if desired.

*Nutritional Information (Per Serving): Calories: 180  Protein: 5g  Carbs: 6g  Fats: 15g  Fiber: 2g  Cholesterol: 5mg  Sodium: 200mg  Potassium: 600mg*

---

# Eggplant Parmesan

**Prep Time: 15 minutes    Cook Time: 40 minutes    Servings: 4**

## INGREDIENTS

- 2 large eggplants, sliced into 1/2-inch rounds
- 1 tsp salt
- 1 cup almond flour
- 1 cup grated Parmesan cheese
- 2 tsp Italian seasoning
- 2 large eggs, beaten
- 2 cups marinara sauce (sugar-free)
- 2 cups shredded mozzarella cheese
- 1/4 cup fresh basil, chopped
- 2 tbsp olive oil

## COOKING PROCESS

1. Preheat Oven: Preheat to 375°F (190°C).
2. Prepare Eggplant: Salt eggplant slices and let sit for 15 minutes. Pat dry.
3. Bread Eggplant: Mix almond flour, Parmesan, and Italian seasoning. Dip eggplant in eggs, then coat with almond flour mixture.
4. Bake Eggplant: Brown eggplant slices in olive oil, then bake on a sheet for 20 minutes.
5. Assemble Dish: Layer marinara sauce, eggplant, and mozzarella in a baking dish. Repeat layers, ending with mozzarella.
6. Bake: Bake for 20 minutes until cheese is bubbly.
7. Serve: Garnish with basil and serve hot.

*Nutritional Information (Per Serving): Calories: 350  Protein: 20g  Carbs: 10g  Fats: 25g  Fiber: 6g  Cholesterol: 100mg  Sodium: 600mg  Potassium: 800mg*

# Cauliflower Crust Margherita Pizza

**Prep Time: 15 minutes    Cook Time: 25 minutes    Servings: 2**

## INGREDIENTS

Crust:

- 1 medium cauliflower head, grated (4 cups)
- 1/2 cup shredded mozzarella
- 1/4 cup grated Parmesan
- 1 egg
- 1 tsp dried oregano
- 1/2 tsp garlic powder
- Salt and pepper

Topping:

- 1/2 cup sugar-free marinara sauce
- 1 cup fresh mozzarella, sliced
- 1/2 cup cherry tomatoes, halved
- Fresh basil leaves
- 1 tbsp olive oil
- Salt and pepper

## COOKING PROCESS

1. Preheat Oven: Preheat to 400°F (200°C). Line a baking sheet with parchment paper.
2. Prepare Crust: Mix grated cauliflower, mozzarella, Parmesan, egg, oregano, garlic powder, salt, and pepper. Form into a crust on the baking sheet.
3. Bake Crust: Bake for 15-20 minutes until golden and firm.
4. Add Toppings: Spread marinara sauce, add mozzarella slices and cherry tomatoes.
5. Bake Pizza: Bake for another 10 minutes until cheese melts.
6. Garnish: Drizzle with olive oil, sprinkle with salt and pepper, and top with basil leaves.
7. Serve: Slice and serve hot.

*Nutritional Information (Per Serving): Calories: 250  Protein: 15g  Carbs: 12g  Fats: 18g  Fiber: 5g  Cholesterol: 80mg Sodium: 600mg  Potassium: 700mg*

---

# Stuffed Bell Peppers with Quinoa and Cheese

**Prep Time: 15 minutes    Cook Time: 30 minutes    Servings: 4**

## INGREDIENTS

- 4 bell peppers, tops cut off and seeds removed
- 1 cup cooked quinoa
- 1 cup black beans, drained and rinsed
- 1 cup corn kernels (fresh or frozen)
- 1 cup shredded cheddar cheese
- 1/2 cup diced tomatoes
- 1/4 cup chopped cilantro
- 1 tsp cumin
- 1/2 tsp chili powder
- Salt and pepper to taste

## COOKING PROCESS

1. Preheat Oven: Preheat to 375°F (190°C).
2. Prepare Filling: In a large bowl, combine cooked quinoa, black beans, corn, 1/2 cup shredded cheese, diced tomatoes, cilantro, cumin, chili powder, salt, and pepper.
3. Stuff Peppers: Fill each bell pepper with the quinoa mixture. Place stuffed peppers in a baking dish.
4. Bake: Cover with foil and bake for 20 minutes. Remove foil, sprinkle remaining cheese on top of peppers, and bake for an additional 10 minutes or until cheese is melted and peppers are tender.
5. Serve: Let cool slightly before serving.

*Nutritional Information (Per Serving): Calories: 250  Protein: 10g  Carbs: 35g  Fats: 9g  Fiber: 8g  Cholesterol: 20mg Sodium: 350mg  Potassium: 500mg*

# Creamy Garlic Mushroom and Spinach Skillet

**Prep Time: 10 minutes****Cook Time: 15 minutes****Servings: 4**

## INGREDIENTS

- 2 tbsp butter
- 1 small onion, diced
- 3 cloves garlic, minced
- 1 lb mushrooms, sliced
- 4 cups fresh spinach
- 1/2 cup heavy cream
- 1/4 cup grated Parmesan cheese
- Salt and pepper to taste
- Optional: chopped parsley for garnish

## COOKING PROCESS

1. Cook Onions and Garlic: In a large skillet, melt butter over medium heat. Add diced onion and garlic, cooking until softened.
2. Cook Mushrooms: Add sliced mushrooms to the skillet. Cook until they release their juices and become tender.
3. Add Spinach: Add fresh spinach to the skillet and cook until wilted.
4. Add Cream and Cheese: Stir in heavy cream and grated Parmesan cheese. Cook until the sauce thickens. Season with salt and pepper to taste.
5. Serve: Garnish with chopped parsley if desired. Serve immediately.

*Nutritional Information (Per Serving): Calories: 200 Protein: 5g Carbs: 7g Fats: 17g Fiber: 2g Cholesterol: 50mg Sodium: 200mg Potassium: 600mg*

---

# Spaghetti Squash Alfredo with Roasted Vegetables

**Prep Time: 15 minutes****Cook Time: 45 minutes****Servings: 4**

## INGREDIENTS

Spaghetti Squash:
- 1 large spaghetti squash
- 2 tbsp olive oil
- Salt and pepper

Roasted Vegetables:
- 1 zucchini, sliced
- 1 red bell pepper, sliced
- 1 yellow bell pepper, sliced
- 1 cup cherry tomatoes
- 2 tbsp olive oil
- Salt and pepper

Alfredo Sauce:
- 2 tbsp butter
- 3 cloves garlic, minced
- 1 cup heavy cream
- 1 cup grated Parmesan cheese
- Salt and pepper
- Optional: parsley for garnish

## COOKING PROCESS

1. Preheat Oven: Preheat to 400°F (200°C).
2. Roast Squash: Halve squash, remove seeds, drizzle with olive oil, season. Roast cut side down for 40-45 minutes. Scrape out strands.
3. Roast Vegetables: Toss vegetables with olive oil, salt, and pepper. Roast for 20-25 minutes.
4. Make Sauce: Melt butter in a skillet over medium heat. Add garlic, cook until fragrant. Stir in cream, simmer. Whisk in Parmesan until thickened. Season.
5. Combine: Toss squash strands and vegetables in the sauce.
6. Serve: Garnish with parsley if desired.

*Nutritional Information (Per Serving): Calories: 350 Protein: 10g Carbs: 15g Fats: 28g Fiber: 5g Cholesterol: 70mg Sodium: 400mg Potassium: 700mg*

# Broccoli Cheddar Soup

**Prep Time: 10 minutes      Cook Time: 20 minutes      Servings: 4**

## INGREDIENTS

- 4 cups broccoli florets
- 1 cup shredded carrots
- 1 small onion, chopped
- 2 cloves garlic, minced
- 4 cups chicken broth
- 1 cup heavy cream
- 2 cups shredded cheddar cheese
- 2 tbsp butter
- 1 tsp mustard powder
- Salt and pepper to taste
- Optional: chopped chives for garnish

## COOKING PROCESS

1. Sauté Vegetables: Melt butter in a pot. Sauté onion and garlic until soft.
2. Add Broccoli and Carrots: Add broccoli and carrots, cook 5 minutes.
3. Simmer: Add broth, simmer 10 minutes until vegetables are tender.
4. Blend: Blend soup until smooth or leave chunky.
5. Add Cream and Cheese: Stir in cream, cheese, mustard powder, salt, and pepper until smooth.
6. Serve: Garnish with chives if desired.

*Nutritional Information (Per Serving): Calories: 320  Protein: 15g  Carbs: 10g  Fats: 25g  Fiber: 3g  Cholesterol: 80mg Sodium: 600mg  Potassium: 400mg*

---

# Roasted Brussels Sprouts with Bacon

**Prep Time: 10 minutes      Cook Time: 25 minutes      Servings: 4**

## INGREDIENTS

- 1 lb Brussels sprouts, trimmed and halved
- 4 slices bacon, chopped
- 2 tbsp olive oil
- Salt and pepper to taste
- Optional: balsamic glaze for drizzling

## COOKING PROCESS

1. Preheat Oven: Preheat to 400°F (200°C).
2. Prepare Brussels Sprouts: Toss Brussels sprouts with olive oil, salt, and pepper.
3. Combine with Bacon: Spread Brussels sprouts on a baking sheet and scatter chopped bacon on top.
4. Roast: Roast for 20-25 minutes until Brussels sprouts are tender and bacon is crispy, stirring halfway through.
5. Serve: Drizzle with balsamic glaze if desired.

*Nutritional Information (Per Serving): Calories: 180  Protein: 6g  Carbs: 10g  Fats: 14g  Fiber: 4g Cholesterol: 15mg  Sodium: 300mg  Potassium: 450mg*

# Cauliflower Fried Rice

**Prep Time: 10 minutes**     **Cook Time: 15 minutes**     **Servings: 4**

## INGREDIENTS

- 4 cups cauliflower rice
- 2 tbsp olive oil
- 1 small onion, chopped
- 2 cloves garlic, minced
- 1 cup mixed vegetables (peas, carrots, bell peppers), chopped
- 2 large eggs, beaten
- 3 tbsp soy sauce (or tamari)
- 1 tbsp sesame oil
- 1/4 cup green onions, sliced
- Salt and pepper to taste

## COOKING PROCESS

1. Cook Onion and Garlic: Sauté onion and garlic in olive oil until soft.
2. Add Vegetables: Add mixed vegetables, cook 3-4 minutes.
3. Cook Cauliflower Rice: Add cauliflower rice, cook 5-7 minutes.
4. Scramble Eggs: Push mixture aside, scramble eggs in the skillet.
5. Combine: Stir in soy sauce, sesame oil, salt, and pepper. Cook 2 minutes.
6. Serve: Garnish with green onions.

*Nutritional Information (Per Serving): Calories: 150  Protein: 6g  Carbs: 8g  Fats: 11g  Fiber: 3g  Cholesterol: 70mg*
*Sodium: 600mg  Potassium: 300mg*

---

# Stuffed Bell Peppers with Ground Turkey

**Prep Time: 10 minutes**     **Cook Time: 40 minutes**     **Servings: 4**

## INGREDIENTS

- 4 large bell peppers, tops cut off and seeds removed
- 1 lb ground turkey
- 1 small onion, chopped
- 2 cloves garlic, minced
- 1 cup cooked cauliflower rice
- 1 cup shredded mozzarella cheese
- 1 can (14.5 oz) diced tomatoes, drained
- 1 tsp Italian seasoning
- Salt and pepper to taste
- Optional: chopped parsley for garnish

## COOKING PROCESS

1. Preheat Oven: Preheat to 375°F (190°C).
2. Cook Turkey: Brown ground turkey with onion and garlic. Season with salt, pepper, and Italian seasoning.
3. Mix Filling: Combine cooked turkey, cauliflower rice, diced tomatoes, and half the mozzarella cheese.
4. Stuff Peppers: Fill bell peppers with turkey mixture, place in a baking dish.
5. Bake: Cover with foil, bake 30 minutes. Uncover, top with remaining cheese, bake 10 minutes.
6. Serve: Garnish with parsley if desired.

*Nutritional Information (Per Serving): Calories: 250  Protein: 25g  Carbs: 12g  Fats: 12g  Fiber: 3g  Cholesterol: 60mg  Sodium: 450mg  Potassium: 600mg*

# CHAPTER 5: SNACKS AND APPETIZERS

# Spicy Roasted Almonds and Pumpkin Seeds

**Prep Time: 5 minutes**     **Cook Time: 20 minutes**     **Servings: 4**

## INGREDIENTS

- 1 cup raw almonds
- 1 cup raw pumpkin seeds
- 2 tbsp olive oil
- 1 tsp smoked paprika
- 1/2 tsp cayenne pepper
- 1/2 tsp garlic powder
- 1/2 tsp salt

## COOKING PROCESS

1. Preheat Oven: Preheat to 350°F (175°C).
2. Prepare Nuts and Seeds: In a bowl, mix almonds and pumpkin seeds with olive oil, smoked paprika, cayenne pepper, garlic powder, and salt until well coated.
3. Roast: Spread the mixture in a single layer on a baking sheet. Roast for 15-20 minutes, stirring halfway through, until golden and fragrant.
4. Cool and Serve: Let cool before serving.

*Nutritional Information (Per Serving): Calories: 250  Protein: 8g  Carbs: 8g  Fats: 22g  Fiber: 4g*
*Cholesterol: 0mg  Sodium: 200mg  Potassium: 300mg*

---

# Cinnamon Pecan and Walnut Trail Mix

**Prep Time: 5 minutes**     **Cook Time: 15 minutes**     **Servings: 4**

## INGREDIENTS

- 1 cup pecans
- 1 cup walnuts
- 2 tbsp coconut oil, melted
- 1 tbsp ground cinnamon
- 1 tbsp erythritol or your preferred keto-friendly sweetener
- 1/2 tsp vanilla extract
- 1/4 tsp salt

## COOKING PROCESS

1. Preheat Oven: Preheat to 350°F (175°C).
2. Prepare Nuts: In a bowl, mix pecans and walnuts with melted coconut oil, cinnamon, erythritol, vanilla extract, and salt until well coated.
3. Roast: Spread the mixture in a single layer on a baking sheet. Roast for 12-15 minutes, stirring halfway through, until nuts are toasted.
4. Cool and Serve: Let cool before serving.

*Nutritional Information (Per Serving): Calories: 300  Protein: 5g  Carbs: 5g  Fats: 30g  Fiber: 3g  Cholesterol: 0mg*
*Sodium: 150mg  Potassium: 200mg*

# Savory Herb Cashew and Sunflower Seed Mix

**Prep Time: 5 minutes     Cook Time: 15 minutes     Servings: 4**

## INGREDIENTS

- 1 cup cashews
- 1 cup sunflower seeds
- 2 tbsp olive oil
- 1 tsp dried rosemary
- 1 tsp dried thyme
- 1/2 tsp garlic powder
- 1/2 tsp onion powder
- 1/2 tsp salt
- 1/4 tsp black pepper

## COOKING PROCESS

1. Preheat Oven: Preheat to 350°F (175°C).
2. Prepare Mix: In a bowl, mix cashews and sunflower seeds with olive oil, rosemary, thyme, garlic powder, onion powder, salt, and pepper until well coated.
3. Roast: Spread the mixture in a single layer on a baking sheet. Roast for 12-15 minutes, stirring halfway through, until golden and fragrant.
4. Cool and Serve: Let cool before serving.

*Nutritional Information (Per Serving): Calories: 280  Protein: 8g  Carbs: 10g  Fats: 24g  Fiber: 3g  Cholesterol: 0mg  Sodium: 250mg  Potassium: 300mg*

---

# Coconut Flaxseed and Chia Seed Crunch

**Prep Time: 5 minutes     Cook Time: 15 minutes     Servings: 4**

## INGREDIENTS

- 1 cup pecans
- 1 cup walnuts
- 2 tbsp coconut oil, melted
- 1 tbsp ground cinnamon
- 1 tbsp erythritol or your preferred keto-friendly sweetener
- 1/2 tsp vanilla extract
- 1/4 tsp salt

## COOKING PROCESS

1. Preheat Oven: Preheat to 350°F (175°C).
2. Prepare Nuts: In a bowl, mix pecans and walnuts with melted coconut oil, cinnamon, erythritol, vanilla extract, and salt until well coated.
3. Roast: Spread the mixture in a single layer on a baking sheet. Roast for 12-15 minutes, stirring halfway through, until nuts are toasted.
4. Cool and Serve: Let cool before serving.

*Nutritional Information (Per Serving): Calories: 300  Protein: 5g  Carbs: 5g  Fats: 30g  Fiber: 3g  Cholesterol: 0mg  Sodium: 150mg  Potassium: 200mg*

# Rosemary Garlic Almonds and Pecans

**Prep Time: 5 minutes      Cook Time: 15 minutes      Servings: 4**

## INGREDIENTS

- 1 cup almonds
- 1 cup pecans
- 2 tbsp olive oil
- 1 tbsp fresh rosemary, chopped
- 2 cloves garlic, minced
- 1/2 tsp salt
- 1/4 tsp black pepper

## COOKING PROCESS

1. Preheat Oven: Preheat to 350°F (175°C).
2. Mix Ingredients: In a bowl, combine almonds, pecans, olive oil, rosemary, garlic, salt, and pepper. Mix until nuts are evenly coated.
3. Bake: Spread the nut mixture in a single layer on a baking sheet. Bake for 12-15 minutes, stirring halfway through, until nuts are golden and fragrant.
4. Cool: Let cool before serving.

*Nutritional Information (Per Serving): Calories: 250  Protein: 5g  Carbs: 7g  Fats: 23g  Fiber: 4g  Cholesterol: 0mg Sodium: 150mg  Potassium: 200mg*

---

# Maple Vanilla Macadamia and Hemp Seed Mix

**Prep Time: 5 minutes      Cook Time: 15 minutes      Servings: 4**

## INGREDIENTS

- 1 cup macadamia nuts
- 1/2 cup hemp seeds
- 2 tbsp coconut oil, melted
- 1 tbsp sugar-free maple syrup
- 1 tsp vanilla extract
- 1/4 tsp salt

## COOKING PROCESS

1. Preheat Oven: Preheat to 325°F (165°C).
2. Mix Ingredients: In a bowl, combine macadamia nuts, hemp seeds, melted coconut oil, sugar-free maple syrup, vanilla extract, and salt. Mix until nuts and seeds are evenly coated.
3. Bake: Spread the mixture in a single layer on a baking sheet. Bake for 12-15 minutes, stirring halfway through, until nuts are golden.
4. Cool: Let cool before serving.

*Nutritional Information (Per Serving): Calories: 220  Protein: 4g  Carbs: 5g  Fats: 20g  Fiber: 3g Cholesterol: 0mg  Sodium: 100mg  Potassium: 150mg*

# Smoky Paprika Walnuts and Pumpkin Seeds

**Prep Time: 5 minutes     Cook Time: 15 minutes     Servings: 4**

## INGREDIENTS

- 1 cup walnuts
- 1 cup pumpkin seeds
- 2 tbsp olive oil
- 1 tsp smoked paprika
- 1/2 tsp garlic powder
- 1/2 tsp salt
- 1/4 tsp black pepper

## COOKING PROCESS

1. Preheat Oven: Preheat to 350°F (175°C).
2. Mix Ingredients: In a bowl, combine almonds, pecans, olive oil, rosemary, garlic, salt, and pepper. Mix until nuts are evenly coated.
3. Bake: Spread the nut mixture in a single layer on a baking sheet. Bake for 12-15 minutes, stirring halfway through, until nuts are golden and fragrant.
4. Cool: Let cool before serving.

*Nutritional Information (Per Serving): Calories: 200  Protein: 5g  Carbs: 4g  Fats: 18g  Fiber: 3g  Cholesterol: 0mg*
*Sodium: 150mg  Potassium: 200mg*

---

# Lemon Zest Almond and Flaxseed Blend

**Prep Time: 5 minutes     Cook Time: 15 minutes     Servings: 4**

## INGREDIENTS

- 1 cup almonds
- 1/2 cup flaxseeds
- 2 tbsp olive oil
- Zest of 1 lemon
- 1 tbsp lemon juice
- 1 tbsp erythritol or your preferred keto-friendly sweetener
- 1/2 tsp salt

## COOKING PROCESS

1. Preheat Oven: Preheat to 325°F (165°C).
2. Mix Ingredients: In a bowl, combine almonds, flaxseeds, olive oil, lemon zest, lemon juice, erythritol, and salt. Mix until nuts and seeds are evenly coated.
3. Bake: Spread the mixture in a single layer on a baking sheet. Bake for 12-15 minutes, stirring halfway through, until nuts are golden and fragrant.
4. Cool: Let cool before serving.

*Nutritional Information (Per Serving): Calories: 180  Protein: 5g  Carbs: 6g  Fats: 16g  Fiber: 4g  Cholesterol: 0mg*
*Sodium: 150mg  Potassium: 200mg*

# Italian Antipasto Platter with Mozzarella and Prosciutto

**Prep Time: 10 minutes**     **Cook Time: 0 minutes**     **Servings: 4**

## INGREDIENTS

- 8 oz fresh mozzarella, sliced
- 8 oz prosciutto, thinly sliced
- 1 cup cherry tomatoes, halved
- 1/2 cup marinated artichoke hearts
- 1/2 cup black olives
- 1/2 cup green olives
- 1/4 cup roasted red peppers, sliced
- 1/4 cup fresh basil leaves
- 2 tbsp olive oil
- 1 tbsp balsamic glaze (optional)
- Salt and pepper to taste

## COOKING PROCESS

1. Arrange Platter: On a large serving platter, arrange mozzarella slices, prosciutto, cherry tomatoes, artichoke hearts, black olives, green olives, roasted red peppers, and fresh basil leaves.
2. Drizzle: Drizzle olive oil over the platter. Add balsamic glaze if desired.
3. Season: Sprinkle with salt and pepper to taste.
4. Serve: Serve immediately, or chill until ready to serve.

*Nutritional Information (Per Serving): Calories: 350  Protein: 20g  Carbs: 6g  Fats: 28g  Fiber: 2g*
*Cholesterol: 70mg  Sodium: 900mg  Potassium: 400mg*

## Cheddar and Salami Snack Platter

**Prep Time: 10 minutes**     **Cook Time: 0 minutes**     **Servings: 4**

## INGREDIENTS

- 8 oz cheddar cheese, sliced
- 8 oz salami, thinly sliced
- 1/2 cup mixed nuts (almonds, walnuts, pecans)
- 1/2 cup green olives
- 1/2 cup cherry tomatoes
- 1/4 cup sliced cucumbers
- 1/4 cup whole grain mustard
- Optional: fresh herbs for garnish

## COOKING PROCESS

1. Arrange Platter: On a large serving platter, arrange cheddar cheese slices, salami, mixed nuts, green olives, cherry tomatoes, and sliced cucumbers.
2. Add Mustard: Place whole grain mustard in a small bowl and add to the platter.
3. Garnish: Garnish with fresh herbs if desired.
4. Serve: Serve immediately.

*Nutritional Information (Per Serving): Calories: 400  Protein: 20g  Carbs: 6g  Fats: 34g  Fiber: 2g*
*Cholesterol: 70mg  Sodium: 1000mg  Potassium: 300mg*

# Greek Mezze Platter with Feta and Olives

**Prep Time: 10 minutes**     **Cook Time: 0 minutes**     **Servings: 4**

## INGREDIENTS

- 8 oz feta cheese, cubed
- 1 cup kalamata olives
- 1 cup cherry tomatoes, halved
- 1 cucumber, sliced
- 1/2 cup roasted red peppers, sliced
- 1/4 cup red onion, thinly sliced
- 1/4 cup fresh parsley, chopped
- 2 tbsp olive oil
- 1 tbsp red wine vinegar
- 1 tsp dried oregano
- Salt and pepper to taste
- Optional: pita bread or low-carb crackers

## COOKING PROCESS

1. Arrange Platter: Arrange feta, olives, tomatoes, cucumber, roasted peppers, and red onion on a platter.
2. Drizzle: Mix olive oil, vinegar, oregano, salt, and pepper. Drizzle over the platter.
3. Garnish: Sprinkle with parsley.
4. Serve: Serve with pita bread or low-carb crackers if desired.

*Nutritional Information (Per Serving): Calories: 300  Protein: 10g  Carbs: 8g  Fats: 24g  Fiber: 3g*
*Cholesterol: 40mg  Sodium: 900mg  Potassium: 400mg*

---

# Swiss and Roast Beef Roll-Ups

**Prep Time: 10 minutes**     **Cook Time: 0 minutes**     **Servings: 4**

## INGREDIENTS

- 8 slices roast beef
- 8 slices Swiss cheese
- 1/4 cup Dijon mustard
- 1/4 cup mayonnaise
- 1 cup baby spinach leaves
- 1/4 cup red bell pepper, thinly sliced

## COOKING PROCESS

1. Prepare Roll-Ups: Lay a slice of roast beef on a flat surface. Spread a thin layer of Dijon mustard and mayonnaise on the beef.
2. Add Fillings: Place a slice of Swiss cheese on the roast beef, followed by a few spinach leaves and a couple of red bell pepper slices.
3. Roll: Roll up the beef tightly around the fillings.
4. Serve: Serve immediately or refrigerate until ready to serve.

*Nutritional Information (Per Serving): Calories: 250  Protein: 20g  Carbs: 3g  Fats: 18g  Fiber: 1g*
*Cholesterol: 60mg  Sodium: 700mg  Potassium: 300mg*

# Pepper Jack and Turkey Platter

**Prep Time: 10 minutes    Cook Time: 0 minutes    Servings: 4**

## INGREDIENTS

- 8 oz sliced turkey breast
- 8 oz pepper jack cheese, sliced
- 1/2 cup mixed olives
- 1/2 cup cherry tomatoes
- 1/2 cup cucumber slices
- 1/4 cup roasted almonds
- Optional: fresh herbs for garnish

## COOKING PROCESS

1. Arrange Ingredients: On a large platter, arrange sliced turkey breast and pepper jack cheese.
2. Add Vegetables and Nuts: Surround with mixed olives, cherry tomatoes, cucumber slices, and roasted almonds.
3. Garnish: Add fresh herbs for garnish if desired.
4. Serve: Serve immediately.

*Nutritional Information (Per Serving): Calories: 300  Protein: 25g  Carbs: 5g  Fats: 20g  Fiber: 2g*
*Cholesterol: 60mg  Sodium: 800mg  Potassium: 400mg*

---

# Brie and Smoked Salmon Platter

**Prep Time: 10 minutes    Cook Time: 0 minutes    Servings: 4**

## INGREDIENTS

- 8 oz brie cheese, sliced
- 8 oz smoked salmon
- 1/2 cup mixed olives
- 1/2 cup cherry tomatoes
- 1/2 cup cucumber slices
- 1/4 cup capers
- Optional: fresh dill or chives for garnish
- Crackers or keto-friendly bread (optional)

## COOKING PROCESS

1. Arrange Ingredients: On a large platter, arrange sliced brie cheese and smoked salmon.
2. Add Vegetables and Capers: Surround with mixed olives, cherry tomatoes, cucumber slices,  and capers.
3. Garnish: Add fresh dill or chives for garnish if desired.
4. Serve: Serve immediately with crackers or keto-friendly bread if desired.

*Nutritional Information (Per Serving): Calories: 300  Protein: 15g  Carbs: 5g  Fats: 25g  Fiber: 2g*
*Cholesterol: 70mg  Sodium: 700mg  Potassium: 300mg*

# Creamy Avocado and Spinach Dip

**Prep Time: 10 minutes**     **Cook Time: 0 minutes**     **Servings: 4**

## INGREDIENTS

- 2 ripe avocados, peeled and pitted
- 2 cups fresh spinach leaves
- 1/2 cup Greek yogurt
- 1/4 cup fresh cilantro
- 2 cloves garlic, minced
- Juice of 1 lime
- Salt and pepper to taste
- Optional: red pepper flakes for garnish

## COOKING PROCESS

1. Blend Ingredients: In a food processor, combine avocados, spinach, Greek yogurt, cilantro, garlic, lime juice, salt, and pepper. Blend until smooth.
2. Adjust Seasoning: Taste and adjust seasoning if necessary.
3. Serve: Transfer to a bowl, garnish with red pepper flakes if desired, and serve immediately with vegetables or low-carb crackers.

*Nutritional Information (Per Serving): Calories: 180  Protein: 5g  Carbs: 8g  Fats: 15g  Fiber: 6g Cholesterol: 5mg  Sodium: 150mg  Potassium: 600mg*

---

# Smoky Bacon and Cheddar Cheese Spread

**Prep Time: 10 minutes**     **Cook Time: 10 minutes**     **Servings: 4**

## INGREDIENTS

- 8 slices bacon, cooked and crumbled
- 1 cup sharp cheddar cheese, shredded
- 1/2 cup cream cheese, softened
- 1/4 cup sour cream
- 1/4 cup mayonnaise
- 2 green onions, finely chopped
- 1 tsp smoked paprika
- Salt and pepper to taste

## COOKING PROCESS

1. Prepare Bacon: Cook bacon until crispy, then crumble and set aside.
2. Mix Ingredients: In a bowl, combine cheddar cheese, cream cheese, sour cream, mayonnaise, green onions, smoked paprika, salt, and pepper. Mix until well combined.
3. Fold in Bacon: Gently fold in crumbled bacon.
4. Serve: Transfer to a serving dish and serve with low-carb crackers or vegetables.

*Nutritional Information (Per Serving): Calories: 250  Protein: 10g  Carbs: 2g  Fats: 22g  Fiber: 0g Cholesterol: 50mg  Sodium: 450mg  Potassium: 150mg*

# Garlic and Herb Cream Cheese Dip

**Prep Time: 10 minutes     Cook Time: 0 minutes     Servings: 4**

## INGREDIENTS

- 8 oz cream cheese, softened
- 1/4 cup sour cream
- 2 cloves garlic, minced
- 2 tbsp fresh parsley, chopped
- 1 tbsp fresh chives, chopped
- 1 tbsp fresh dill, chopped
- 1 tsp lemon juice
- Salt and pepper to taste

## COOKING PROCESS

1. Mix Ingredients: In a bowl, combine cream cheese, sour cream, garlic, parsley, chives, dill, and lemon juice. Mix until smooth and well combined.
2. Season: Add salt and pepper to taste.
3. Serve: Transfer to a serving dish and serve with low-carb crackers or fresh vegetables.

*Nutritional Information (Per Serving): Calories: 150  Protein: 3g  Carbs: 2g  Fats: 14g  Fiber: 0g*
*Cholesterol: 40mg  Sodium: 150mg  Potassium: 100mg*

---

# Spicy Jalapeno and Artichoke Dip

**Prep Time: 10 minutes     Cook Time: 20 minutes     Servings: 4**

## INGREDIENTS

- 1 can (14 oz) artichoke hearts, drained and chopped
- 1/2 cup mayonnaise
- 1/2 cup sour cream
- 1 cup shredded mozzarella cheese
- 1/2 cup grated Parmesan cheese
- 2 jalapenos, seeded and finely chopped
- 2 cloves garlic, minced
- 1 tsp smoked paprika
- Salt and pepper to taste
- Optional: chopped fresh parsley for garnish

## COOKING PROCESS

1. Preheat Oven: Preheat to 375°F (190°C).
2. Mix Ingredients: In a bowl, combine chopped artichoke hearts, mayonnaise, sour cream, mozzarella cheese, Parmesan cheese, jalapenos, garlic, smoked paprika, salt, and pepper. Mix until well combined.
3. Bake: Transfer the mixture to a baking dish. Bake for 20 minutes or until the top is golden and bubbly.
4. Serve: Garnish with chopped parsley if desired and serve hot with low-carb crackers or fresh vegetables.

*Nutritional Information (Per Serving): Calories: 250  Protein: 10g  Carbs: 5g  Fats: 22g  Fiber: 2g*
*Cholesterol: 50mg  Sodium: 400mg  Potassium: 200mg*

# Sun-Dried Tomato and Olive Tapenade

**Prep Time: 10 minutes    Cook Time: 0 minutes    Servings: 4**

## INGREDIENTS

- 1 cup pitted black olives
- 1/2 cup sun-dried tomatoes in oil, drained
- 2 cloves garlic
- 2 tbsp capers
- 1/4 cup fresh parsley
- 3 tbsp olive oil
- 1 tbsp lemon juice
- Salt and pepper to taste

## COOKING PROCESS

1. Blend Ingredients: In a food processor, combine olives, sun-dried tomatoes, garlic, capers, and parsley. Pulse until coarsely chopped.
2. Add Olive Oil and Lemon Juice: Add olive oil and lemon juice. Pulse until combined but still slightly chunky.
3. Season: Season with salt and pepper to taste.
4. Serve: Serve immediately with crackers, bread, or as a topping for grilled meats.

*Nutritional Information (Per Serving): Calories: 150  Protein: 2g  Carbs: 5g  Fats: 14g  Fiber: 2g*
*Cholesterol: 0mg  Sodium: 400mg  Potassium: 200mg*

---

# Roasted Red Pepper and Walnut Dip

**Prep Time: 10 minutes    Cook Time: 10 minutes    Servings: 4**

## INGREDIENTS

- 2 large roasted red peppers, peeled and chopped
- 1/2 cup walnuts
- 2 cloves garlic
- 2 tbsp olive oil
- 1 tbsp lemon juice
- 1 tsp ground cumin
- Salt and pepper to taste
- Optional: fresh parsley for garnish

## COOKING PROCESS

1. Toast Walnuts: In a dry skillet over medium heat, toast walnuts until fragrant, about 5 minutes. Let cool.
2. Blend Ingredients: In a food processor, combine roasted red peppers, toasted walnuts, garlic, olive oil, lemon juice, and ground cumin. Blend until smooth.
3. Season: Season with salt and pepper to taste.
4. Serve: Transfer to a serving bowl and garnish with fresh parsley if desired. Serve with pita bread, crackers, or fresh vegetables.

*Nutritional Information (Per Serving): Calories: 170  Protein: 3g  Carbs: 7g  Fats: 15g  Fiber: 3g*
*Cholesterol: 0mg  Sodium: 150mg  Potassium: 250mg*

# Creamy Blue Cheese Dip

**Prep Time: 10 minutes     Cook Time: 0 minutes     Servings: 4**

## INGREDIENTS

- 1/2 cup sour cream
- 1/4 cup mayonnaise
- 1/4 cup crumbled blue cheese
- 1 clove garlic, minced
- 1 tbsp lemon juice
- 1/2 tsp Worcestershire sauce
- Salt and pepper to taste
- Optional: chopped chives for garnish

## COOKING PROCESS

1. Mix Ingredients: In a bowl, combine sour cream, mayonnaise, blue cheese, minced garlic, lemon juice, and Worcestershire sauce. Mix well.
2. Season: Season with salt and pepper to taste.
3. Chill: Refrigerate for at least 30 minutes to allow the flavors to meld.
4. Serve: Transfer to a serving bowl and garnish with chopped chives if desired. Serve with vegetables, crackers, or wings.

*Nutritional Information (Per Serving): Calories: 180  Protein: 2g  Carbs: 2g  Fats: 18g  Fiber: 0g Cholesterol: 20mg  Sodium: 250mg  Potassium: 50mg*

---

# Keto Pimento Cheese Spread

**Prep Time: 10 minutes     Cook Time: 0 minutes     Servings: 4**

## INGREDIENTS

- 1 cup shredded cheddar cheese
- 1/2 cup mayonnaise
- 1/4 cup diced pimentos, drained
- 1/4 tsp garlic powder
- 1/4 tsp onion powder
- Salt and pepper to taste
- Optional: 1/4 tsp smoked paprika

## COOKING PROCESS

1. Mix Ingredients: In a bowl, combine shredded cheddar cheese, mayonnaise, diced pimentos, garlic powder, onion powder, and smoked paprika if using. Mix well.
2. Season: Season with salt and pepper to taste.
3. Chill: Refrigerate for at least 30 minutes to allow the flavors to meld.
4. Serve: Serve with vegetables, low-carb crackers, or use as a spread for sandwiches.

*Nutritional Information (Per Serving): Calories: 250  Protein: 5g  Carbs: 1g  Fats: 24g  Fiber: 0g Cholesterol: 25mg  Sodium: 350mg  Potassium: 50mg*

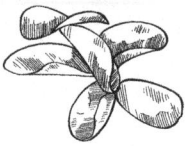

# Zucchini Parmesan Crisps

**Prep Time: 10 minutes**     **Cook Time: 20 minutes**     **Servings: 4**

## INGREDIENTS

- 2 medium zucchinis, sliced into thin rounds
- 1/2 cup grated Parmesan cheese
- 1/2 cup almond flour
- 1 tsp garlic powder
- 1 tsp Italian seasoning
- Salt and pepper to taste
- 1 large egg, beaten
- Optional: marinara sauce for dipping

## COOKING PROCESS

1. Preheat Oven: Preheat to 425°F (220°C). Line a baking sheet with parchment paper.
2. Prepare Coating: In a bowl, combine Parmesan cheese, almond flour, garlic powder, Italian seasoning, salt, and pepper.
3. Coat Zucchini: Dip zucchini slices into the beaten egg, then coat with the Parmesan mixture. Place on the prepared baking sheet.
4. Bake: Bake for 15-20 minutes, flipping halfway through, until golden and crispy.
5. Serve: Serve hot with marinara sauce if desired.

*Nutritional Information (Per Serving): Calories: 150  Protein: 8g  Carbs: 4g  Fats: 11g  Fiber: 2g*
*Cholesterol: 50mg  Sodium: 300mg  Potassium: 300mg*

---

# Mini Bacon-Wrapped Meatballs

**Prep Time: 15 minutes**     **Cook Time: 25 minutes**     **Servings: 4**

## INGREDIENTS

- 1 lb ground beef
- 1/2 cup grated Parmesan cheese
- 1/4 cup almond flour
- 1 large egg
- 2 cloves garlic, minced
- 1 tsp Italian seasoning
- Salt and pepper to taste
- 8 slices bacon, cut in half

## COOKING PROCESS

1. Preheat Oven: Preheat to 400°F (200°C). Line a baking sheet with parchment paper.
2. Prepare Meatballs: In a bowl, combine ground beef, Parmesan cheese, almond flour, egg, garlic, Italian seasoning, salt, and pepper. Mix until well combined.
3. Form Meatballs: Shape the mixture into small meatballs, about 1 inch in diameter.
4. Wrap with Bacon: Wrap each meatball with a half slice of bacon and secure with a toothpick.
5. Bake: Place the meatballs on the prepared baking sheet. Bake for 20-25 minutes until the bacon is crispy and the meatballs are cooked through.
6. Serve: Serve hot.

*Nutritional Information (Per Serving): Calories: 350  Protein: 20g  Carbs: 3g  Fats: 28g  Fiber: 1g*
*Cholesterol: 90mg  Sodium: 600mg  Potassium: 400mg*

# Cheesy Cauliflower Tots

**Prep Time: 15 minutes    Cook Time: 25 minutes    Servings: 4**

## INGREDIENTS

- 3 cups cauliflower florets
- 1 cup shredded cheddar cheese
- 1/4 cup grated Parmesan cheese
- 1/4 cup almond flour
- 1 large egg, beaten
- 1/2 tsp garlic powder
- 1/2 tsp onion powder
- Salt and pepper to taste

## COOKING PROCESS

1. Preheat Oven: Preheat to 400°F (200°C). Line a baking sheet with parchment paper.
2. Prepare Cauliflower: Steam or microwave cauliflower until tender. Drain and finely chop or pulse in a food processor.
3. Mix Ingredients: Combine cauliflower, cheddar, Parmesan, almond flour, egg, garlic powder, onion powder, salt, and pepper in a bowl.
4. Form Tots: Shape mixture into small tots, place on the baking sheet.
5. Bake: Bake for 20-25 minutes, turning halfway, until golden and crispy.
6. Serve: Serve hot with your favorite dipping sauce.

*Nutritional Information (Per Serving): Calories: 150  Protein: 8g  Carbs: 6g  Fats: 10g  Fiber: 2g*
*Cholesterol: 60mg  Sodium: 300mg  Potassium: 300mg*

---

# Stuffed Mushroom Caps with Sausage and Cream Cheese

**Prep Time: 15 minutes    Cook Time: 20 minutes    Servings: 4**

## INGREDIENTS

- 16 large mushroom caps, stems removed
- 1/2 lb sausage, crumbled and cooked
- 8 oz cream cheese, softened
- 1/4 cup grated Parmesan cheese
- 2 cloves garlic, minced
- 1/4 cup fresh parsley, chopped
- Salt and pepper to taste
- Optional: fresh parsley for garnish

## COOKING PROCESS

1. Preheat Oven: Preheat to 375°F (190°C). Line a baking sheet with parchment paper.
2. Prepare Filling: In a bowl, combine cooked sausage, cream cheese, Parmesan cheese, garlic, chopped parsley, salt, and pepper. Mix until well combined.
3. Stuff Mushrooms: Spoon the sausage mixture into each mushroom cap, filling generously.
4. Bake: Place stuffed mushrooms on the baking sheet. Bake for 20 minutes, or until mushrooms are tender and the filling is golden.
5. Serve: Garnish with additional parsley if desired and serve hot.

*Nutritional Information (Per Serving): Calories: 250  Protein: 12g  Carbs: 6g  Fats: 20g  Fiber: 1g*
*Cholesterol: 60mg  Sodium: 500mg  Potassium: 400mg*

# Bacon and Cheddar Stuffed Jalapenos

**Prep Time: 10 minutes**      **Cook Time: 20 minutes**      **Servings: 4**

## INGREDIENTS

- 8 large jalapenos, halved and seeded
- 4 slices bacon, cooked and crumbled
- 1 cup shredded cheddar cheese
- 4 oz cream cheese, softened
- 1/4 tsp garlic powder
- 1/4 tsp onion powder
- Salt and pepper to taste
- Optional: chopped fresh parsley for garnish

## COOKING PROCESS

1. Preheat Oven: Preheat to 400°F (200°C). Line a baking sheet with parchment paper.
2. Prepare Filling: In a bowl, mix together crumbled bacon, cheddar cheese, cream cheese, garlic powder, onion powder, salt, and pepper.
3. Stuff Jalapenos: Spoon the cheese mixture into each jalapeno half.
4. Bake: Place the stuffed jalapenos on the prepared baking sheet. Bake for 15-20 minutes, until the jalapenos are tender and the cheese is melted and bubbly.
5. Serve: Garnish with chopped fresh parsley if desired. Serve hot.

*Nutritional Information (Per Serving): Calories: 250 Protein: 8g Carbs: 4g Fats: 22g Fiber: 1g*
*Cholesterol: 50mg Sodium: 400mg Potassium: 150mg*

---

# Keto Chicken Tenders

**Prep Time: 15 minutes**      **Cook Time: 20 minutes**      **Servings: 4**

## INGREDIENTS

- 1 lb chicken tenders
- 1 cup almond flour
- 1/2 cup grated Parmesan cheese
- 1 tsp garlic powder
- 1 tsp onion powder
- 1/2 tsp smoked paprika
- Salt and pepper to taste
- 2 large eggs, beaten
- 2 tbsp olive oil or melted butter (for drizzling)

## COOKING PROCESS

1. Preheat Oven: Preheat to 400°F (200°C). Line a baking sheet with parchment paper.
2. Prepare Breading: In a bowl, combine almond flour, Parmesan cheese, garlic powder, onion powder, smoked paprika, salt, and pepper.
3. Coat Chicken: Dip each chicken tender in the beaten eggs, then coat with the almond flour mixture. Place on the prepared baking sheet.
4. Drizzle Oil: Drizzle olive oil or melted butter over the coated chicken tenders.
5. Bake: Bake for 20 minutes, turning halfway through, until the chicken is cooked through and the coating is golden brown.
6. Serve: Serve hot with your favorite keto-friendly dipping sauce.

*Nutritional Information (Per Serving): Calories: 300 Protein: 25g Carbs: 4g Fats: 20g Fiber: 2g*
*Cholesterol: 100mg Sodium: 400mg Potassium: 400mg*

# Garlic Butter Shrimp Skewers

**Prep Time: 10 minutes    Cook Time: 10 minutes    Servings: 4**

## INGREDIENTS

- 1 lb large shrimp, peeled and deveined
- 1/4 cup butter, melted
- 4 cloves garlic, minced
- 2 tbsp fresh parsley, chopped
- 1 tbsp lemon juice
- Salt and pepper to taste
- Skewers

## COOKING PROCESS

1. Preheat Grill: Preheat grill to medium-high heat.
2. Prepare Shrimp: Thread shrimp onto skewers.
3. Make Garlic Butter: In a bowl, combine melted butter, minced garlic, chopped parsley, lemon juice, salt, and pepper.
4. Brush Shrimp: Brush the garlic butter mixture over the shrimp skewers.
5. Grill Shrimp: Grill the shrimp skewers for 2-3 minutes on each side, until shrimp are pink and opaque.
6. Serve: Serve hot with extra garlic butter for dipping if desired.

*Nutritional Information (Per Serving): Calories: 200  Protein: 20g  Carbs: 2g  Fats: 14g  Fiber: 0g*
*Cholesterol: 220mg  Sodium: 400mg  Potassium: 200mg*

---

# Keto Deviled Eggs

**Prep Time: 15 minutes    Cook Time: 0 minutes    Servings: 4**

## INGREDIENTS

- 6 large eggs, hard-boiled and peeled
- 3 tbsp mayonnaise
- 1 tsp Dijon mustard
- 1 tsp apple cider vinegar
- Salt and pepper to taste
- Paprika for garnish
- Optional: chopped chives or bacon bits for garnish

## COOKING PROCESS

1. Prepare Eggs: Slice the hard-boiled eggs in half lengthwise. Remove the yolks and place them in a bowl.
2. Make Filling: Mash the yolks with a fork. Add mayonnaise, Dijon mustard, apple cider vinegar, salt, and pepper. Mix until smooth.
3. Fill Eggs: Spoon or pipe the yolk mixture back into the egg whites.
4. Garnish: Sprinkle with paprika and add chopped chives or bacon bits if desired.
5. Serve: Serve immediately or refrigerate until ready to serve.

*Nutritional Information (Per Serving): Calories: 300  Protein: 25g  Carbs: 4g  Fats: 20g  Fiber: 2g*
*Cholesterol: 100mg  Sodium: 400mg  Potassium: 400mg*

# CHAPTER 6:
# DESSERTS

# Almond Flour Chocolate Chip Cookies

**Prep Time: 10 minutes     Cook Time: 12 minutes     Servings: 24 cookies**

Keto-Friendly Cookies and Bars

## INGREDIENTS

- 2 1/2 cups almond flour
- 1/2 cup butter, melted
- 1/2 cup erythritol
- 1 large egg
- 1 tsp vanilla extract
- 1/2 tsp baking soda
- 1/4 tsp salt
- 1 cup sugar-free chocolate chips

## COOKING PROCESS

1. Preheat Oven: Preheat to 350°F (175°C). Line a baking sheet with parchment paper.
2. Mix Ingredients: Combine melted butter, erythritol, egg, and vanilla. Add almond flour, baking soda, and salt. Mix well.
3. Fold in Chips: Fold in chocolate chips.
4. Form Cookies: Scoop dough onto baking sheet, forming 24 balls. Flatten slightly.
5. Bake: Bake for 10-12 minutes until edges are golden. Cool on sheet, then transfer to a rack.

*Nutritional Information (Per Serving): Calories: 120  Protein: 3g  Carbs: 4g  Fats: 11g  Fiber: 2g*
*Cholesterol: 10mg  Sodium: 50mg  Potassium: 50mg*

---

# Coconut Macadamia Nut Bars

**Prep Time: 10 minutes     Cook Time: 20 minutes     Servings: 16 bars**

## INGREDIENTS

- 2 cups unsweetened shredded coconut
- 1 cup macadamia nuts, chopped
- 1/2 cup almond flour
- 1/4 cup coconut oil, melted
- 1/4 cup erythritol or your preferred keto-friendly sweetener
- 1 large egg
- 1 tsp vanilla extract
- 1/4 tsp salt

## COOKING PROCESS

1. Preheat Oven: Preheat to 350°F (175°C). Line an 8x8-inch baking pan with parchment paper.
2. Mix Ingredients: In a bowl, combine shredded coconut, macadamia nuts, almond flour, coconut oil, erythritol, egg, vanilla extract, and salt. Mix until well combined.
3. Press into Pan: Press the mixture firmly into the prepared baking pan.
4. Bake: Bake for 20 minutes or until the edges are golden brown.
5. Cool and Slice: Let cool completely in the pan before slicing into 16 bars.

*Nutritional Information (Per Serving): Calories: 150  Protein: 2g  Carbs: 4g  Fats: 14g  Fiber: 3g*
*Cholesterol: 10mg  Sodium: 50mg  Potassium: 60mg*

# Peanut Butter Keto Cookies

**Prep Time: 10 minutes     Cook Time: 12 minutes     Servings: 20 cookies**

## INGREDIENTS

- 1 cup peanut butter (no sugar added)
- 1/2 cup erythritol or your preferred keto-friendly sweetener
- 1 large egg
- 1 tsp vanilla extract
- 1/2 tsp baking powder
- 1/4 tsp salt

## COOKING PROCESS

1. Preheat Oven: Preheat to 350°F (175°C). Line a baking sheet with parchment paper.
2. Mix Ingredients: In a bowl, combine peanut butter, erythritol, egg, vanilla extract, baking powder, and salt. Mix until well combined.
3. Form Cookies: Scoop dough onto the baking sheet, forming 20 small balls. Flatten each ball with a fork, creating a crisscross pattern.
4. Bake: Bake for 10-12 minutes or until the edges are golden brown.
5. Cool: Let cookies cool on the baking sheet for a few minutes before transferring to a wire rack to cool completely.

*Nutritional Information (Per Serving): Calories: 110  Protein: 4g  Carbs: 4g  Fats: 9g  Fiber: 2g*
*Cholesterol: 10mg  Sodium: 90mg  Potassium: 100mg*

---

# Lemon Poppy Seed Keto Bars

**Prep Time: 10 minutes     Cook Time: 25 minutes     Servings: 16 bars**

## INGREDIENTS

- 2 cups almond flour
- 1/2 cup erythritol
- 1/4 cup melted coconut oil
- 1/4 cup unsweetened almond milk
- 2 large eggs
- 2 tbsp poppy seeds
- Zest and juice of 1 lemon
- 1 tsp vanilla extract
- 1/2 tsp baking powder
- 1/4 tsp salt

## COOKING PROCESS

1. Preheat Oven: Preheat to 350°F (175°C). Line an 8x8-inch pan with parchment paper.
2. Mix Wet Ingredients: Combine coconut oil, almond milk, eggs, lemon zest, juice, and vanilla.
3. Add Dry Ingredients: Mix in almond flour, erythritol, poppy seeds, baking powder, and salt.
4. Bake: Pour batter into the pan. Bake for 20-25 minutes.
5. Cool and Slice: Cool completely before slicing into bars.

*Nutritional Information (Per Serving): Calories: 120  Protein: 4g  Carbs: 4g  Fats: 10g  Fiber: 2g*
*Cholesterol: 25mg  Sodium: 80mg  Potassium: 60mg*

# Blueberry Almond Flour Muffins

**Prep Time: 10 minutes      Cook Time: 20 minutes      Servings: 12 muffins**

## INGREDIENTS

- 2 1/2 cups almond flour
- 1/2 cup erythritol
- 1/2 tsp baking soda
- 1/4 tsp salt
- 3 large eggs
- 1/4 cup coconut oil, melted
- 1/4 cup unsweetened almond milk
- 1 tsp vanilla extract
- 1 cup fresh blueberries

## COOKING PROCESS

1. Preheat Oven: Preheat to 350°F (175°C). Line a muffin tin with paper liners.
2. Mix Dry Ingredients: In a bowl, combine almond flour, erythritol, baking soda, and salt.
3. Mix Wet Ingredients: In another bowl, whisk together eggs, melted coconut oil, almond milk, and vanilla extract.
4. Combine: Add wet ingredients to dry ingredients and mix until well combined. Fold in blueberries.
5. Bake: Divide the batter evenly among the muffin cups. Bake for 20-25 minutes, or until a toothpick inserted into the center comes out clean.
6. Cool: Let muffins cool in the tin for a few minutes before transferring to a wire rack to cool completely.

*Nutritional Information (Per Serving): Calories: 150  Protein: 5g  Carbs: 6g  Fats: 12g  Fiber: 3g*
*Cholesterol: 40mg  Sodium: 70mg  Potassium: 50mg*

# Chocolate Avocado Cake

**Prep Time: 15 minutes      Cook Time: 30 minutes      Servings: 12**

## INGREDIENTS

- 1 1/2 cups almond flour
- 1/2 cup unsweetened cocoa powder
- 1/2 cup erythritol
- 1 tsp baking soda
- 1/4 tsp salt
- 2 large eggs
- 1 large ripe avocado, mashed
- 1/2 cup coconut oil, melted
- 1/2 cup unsweetened almond milk
- 1 tsp vanilla extract

## COOKING PROCESS

1. Preheat Oven: Preheat to 350°F (175°C). Grease and line an 8-inch cake pan.
2. Mix Dry Ingredients: Combine almond flour, cocoa powder, erythritol, baking soda, and salt.
3. Mix Wet Ingredients: Whisk together eggs, mashed avocado, coconut oil, almond milk, and vanilla.
4. Combine: Mix wet and dry ingredients until smooth.
5. Bake: Pour batter into the pan. Bake 25-30 minutes until a toothpick comes out clean.
6. Cool: Cool in the pan for 10 minutes, then transfer to a rack.

*Nutritional Information (Per Serving): Calories: 180  Protein: 5g  Carbs: 7g  Fats: 15g  Fiber: 4g*
*Cholesterol: 35mg  Sodium: 120mg  Potassium: 200mg*

# Cinnamon Streusel Muffins

**Prep Time: 10 minutes    Cook Time: 20 minutes    Servings: 12 muffins**

## INGREDIENTS

Muffins:

- 2 cups almond flour
- 1/2 cup erythritol
- 1/4 cup coconut oil, melted
- 1/4 cup unsweetened almond milk
- 3 large eggs
- 1 tsp vanilla extract
- 1 tsp baking powder
- 1/2 tsp ground cinnamon
- 1/4 tsp salt

Streusel Topping:

- 1/4 cup almond flour
- 2 tbsp erythritol
- 1 tsp ground cinnamon
- 2 tbsp butter, melted

## COOKING PROCESS

1. Preheat Oven: Preheat to 350°F (175°C). Line a muffin tin with liners.
2. Mix Wet Ingredients: Whisk coconut oil, almond milk, eggs, and vanilla.
3. Mix Dry Ingredients: Combine almond flour, erythritol, baking powder, cinnamon, and salt. Add wet ingredients, mix.
4. Prepare Streusel: Mix almond flour, erythritol, cinnamon, and melted butter until crumbly.
5. Fill Muffin Cups: Divide batter into muffin cups. Top with streusel.
6. Bake: Bake 20-25 minutes until a toothpick comes out clean.
7. Cool: Cool in the tin for a few minutes, then transfer to a rack.

*Nutritional Information (Per Serving): Calories: 160  Protein: 5g  Carbs: 6g  Fats: 14g  Fiber: 3g*
*Cholesterol: 35mg  Sodium: 100mg  Potassium: 50mg*

---

# Lemon Ricotta Pound Cake

**Prep Time: 15 minutes    Cook Time: 50 minutes    Servings: 10**

## INGREDIENTS

- 1 1/2 cups almond flour
- 1/2 cup coconut flour
- 1 cup erythritol
- 1 tsp baking powder
- 1/4 tsp salt
- 3 large eggs
- 1 cup ricotta cheese
- 1/2 cup butter, melted
- Zest and juice of 1 lemon
- 1 tsp vanilla extract

## COOKING PROCESS

1. Preheat Oven: Preheat to 350°F (175°C). Grease and line a loaf pan.
2. Mix Dry Ingredients: Combine almond flour, coconut flour, erythritol, baking powder, and salt.
3. Mix Wet Ingredients: Whisk eggs, ricotta, melted butter, lemon zest, juice, and vanilla.
4. Combine: Mix wet and dry ingredients until smooth.
5. Bake: Pour into pan. Bake 45-50 minutes until a toothpick comes out clean.
6. Cool: Cool in the pan for 10 minutes, then transfer to a rack.

*Nutritional Information (Per Serving): Calories: 250  Protein: 7g  Carbs: 8g  Fats: 20g  Fiber: 3g*
*Cholesterol: 70mg  Sodium: 150mg  Potassium: 100mg*

# Dark Chocolate Almond Clusters

**Prep Time: 10 minutes**     **Cook Time: 30 minutes**     **Servings: 12 clusters**

Sugar-Free Chocolates

## INGREDIENTS

- 1 cup dark chocolate chips (sugar-free)
- 1 cup whole almonds
- 1/4 tsp sea salt (optional)

## COOKING PROCESS

1. Melt Chocolate: Melt dark chocolate chips in a microwave-safe bowl in 30-second intervals, stirring between each, until smooth.
2. Mix Almonds: Stir in whole almonds until fully coated with chocolate.
3. Form Clusters: Drop spoonfuls of the chocolate-coated almonds onto a parchment-lined baking sheet to form clusters.
4. Chill: Sprinkle with sea salt if desired. Chill in the refrigerator for 30 minutes or until set.
5. Serve: Serve immediately or store in an airtight container.

*Nutritional Information (Per Serving): Calories: 100  Protein: 2g  Carbs: 5g  Fats: 8g  Fiber: 2g*
*Cholesterol: 0mg  Sodium: 10mg  Potassium: 100mg*

---

# Sugar-Free Chocolate Truffles

**Prep Time: 15 minutes**     **Chill Time: 1 hour**     **Servings: 15 truffles**

## INGREDIENTS

- 1 cup sugar-free dark chocolate chips
- 1/2 cup heavy cream
- 1/4 cup unsweetened cocoa powder (for coating)
- 1/2 tsp vanilla extract
- Optional: chopped nuts, shredded coconut, or additional cocoa powder for coating

## COOKING PROCESS

1. Heat Cream: In a small saucepan, heat the heavy cream until it just begins to simmer.
2. Melt Chocolate: Place chocolate chips in a heatproof bowl. Pour hot cream over the chocolate and let sit for 2 minutes, then stir until smooth and glossy. Add vanilla extract and mix well.
3. Chill Mixture: Cover the mixture and refrigerate for about 1 hour, or until firm enough to scoop.
4. Form Truffles: Using a small spoon or melon baller, scoop out small amounts of the chocolate mixture and roll into balls.
5. Coat Truffles: Roll each truffle in unsweetened cocoa powder, chopped nuts, shredded coconut, or additional cocoa powder until evenly coated.
6. Chill and Serve: Place the truffles on a baking sheet and refrigerate for at least 30 minutes to set. Serve chilled.

*Nutritional Information (Per Serving): Calories: 70  Protein: 1g  Carbs: 3g  Fats: 6g  Fiber: 1g*
*Cholesterol: 10mg  Sodium: 5mg  Potassium: 60mg*

# Keto Chocolate Bark with Nuts and Seeds
## Prep Time: 10 minutes    Cook Time: 30 minutes    Servings: 12

## INGREDIENTS

- 1 cup sugar-free dark chocolate chips
- 1/4 cup almonds, chopped
- 1/4 cup walnuts, chopped
- 2 tbsp pumpkin seeds
- 2 tbsp sunflower seeds
- 1/4 tsp sea salt (optional)

## COOKING PROCESS

1. Melt Chocolate: Melt the dark chocolate chips in a microwave-safe bowl in 30-second intervals, stirring between each, until smooth.
2. Prepare Baking Sheet: Line a baking sheet with parchment paper.
3. Spread Chocolate: Pour the melted chocolate onto the prepared baking sheet and spread into an even layer.
4. Add Toppings: Sprinkle the chopped almonds, walnuts, pumpkin seeds, and sunflower seeds evenly over the chocolate. Press gently to adhere.
5. Chill: Sprinkle with sea salt if desired. Chill in the refrigerator for 30 minutes or until set.
6. Break into Pieces: Once firm, break the chocolate bark into pieces.

*Nutritional Information (Per Serving): Calories: 100  Protein: 2g  Carbs: 5g  Fats: 8g  Fiber: 2g*
*Cholesterol: 0mg  Sodium: 10mg  Potassium: 100mg*

---

# Coconut Oil Chocolate Fudge
## Prep Time: 10 minutes    Chill Time: 1 hour    Servings: 16 pieces

## INGREDIENTS

- 1/2 cup coconut oil, melted
- 1/2 cup unsweetened cocoa powder
- 1/4 cup erythritol or your preferred keto-friendly sweetener
- 1 tsp vanilla extract
- Pinch of salt
- Optional: chopped nuts or shredded coconut for topping

## COOKING PROCESS

1. Mix Ingredients: In a bowl, combine melted coconut oil, cocoa powder, erythritol, vanilla extract, and salt. Mix until smooth.
2. Pour Mixture: Pour the mixture into a parchment-lined 8x8-inch baking dish.
3. Add Toppings: Sprinkle chopped nuts or shredded coconut on top if desired.
4. Chill: Refrigerate for at least 1 hour or until firm.
5. Cut and Serve: Once set, cut into 16 pieces.

*Nutritional Information (Per Serving): Calories: 80  Protein: 0g  Carbs: 3g  Fats: 8g  Fiber: 1g*
*Cholesterol: 0mg  Sodium: 5mg  Potassium: 50mg*

# Vanilla Bean Keto Ice Cream

**Prep Time: 10 minutes**     **Chill Time: 4 hours**     **Servings: 8**

## INGREDIENTS

- 2 cups heavy cream
- 1 cup unsweetened almond milk
- 1/2 cup erythritol
- 1 vanilla bean, split and seeds scraped
- 1 tsp vanilla extract
- 4 large egg yolks

## COOKING PROCESS

1. Heat Cream: Combine heavy cream, almond milk, erythritol, and vanilla bean seeds in a saucepan. Heat until it simmers, then remove from heat.
2. Temper Eggs: Whisk egg yolks. Gradually add a ladle of the hot cream to yolks, whisking constantly. Pour back into the saucepan.
3. Thicken: Cook over low heat, stirring until thickened (5-7 minutes). Do not boil.
4. Strain and Chill: Strain the mixture, stir in vanilla extract, and cool. Refrigerate for at least 4 hours.
5. Churn: Churn in an ice cream maker according to manufacturer's instructions.
6. Freeze: Freeze in an airtight container for at least 2 hours.

*Nutritional Information (Per Serving): Calories: 200  Protein: 3g  Carbs: 3g  Fats: 20g  Fiber: 0g*
*Cholesterol: 100mg  Sodium: 25mg  Potassium: 60mg*

---

# Chocolate Peanut Butter Swirl Ice Cream

**Prep Time: 10 minutes**     **Chill Time: 4 hours**     **Servings: 8**

## INGREDIENTS

- 2 cups heavy cream
- 1 cup unsweetened almond milk
- 1/2 cup erythritol
- 1/2 cup unsweetened cocoa powder
- 1 tsp vanilla extract
- 4 large egg yolks
- 1/2 cup natural peanut butter

## COOKING PROCESS

1. Heat Cream: Combine heavy cream, almond milk, erythritol, and cocoa powder in a saucepan. Heat until it simmers, then remove from heat.
2. Temper Eggs: Whisk egg yolks. Gradually add hot cream mixture to yolks, whisking constantly. Pour back into saucepan.
3. Thicken: Cook over low heat, stirring until thickened (5-7 minutes). Do not boil.
4. Chill: Strain, stir in vanilla, and cool. Refrigerate 4 hours.
5. Churn: Churn in an ice cream maker.
6. Add Peanut Butter: Transfer to a container, swirl in peanut butter, and freeze for 2 hours.

*Nutritional Information (Per Serving): Calories: 250  Protein: 5g  Carbs: 5g  Fats: 22g  Fiber: 1g*
*Cholesterol: 100mg  Sodium: 40mg  Potassium: 100mg*

# Mint Chocolate Chip Keto Ice Cream

**Prep Time: 10 minutes     Chill Time: 4 hours     Servings:  8**

## INGREDIENTS

- 2 cups heavy cream
- 1 cup unsweetened almond milk
- 1/2 cup erythritol
- 1 tsp vanilla extract
- 1 tsp peppermint extract
- 4 large egg yolks
- 1/2 cup sugar-free chocolate chips
- Optional: green food coloring

## COOKING PROCESS

1. Heat Cream: Combine heavy cream, almond milk, and erythritol. Heat until it simmers, then remove from heat.
2. Temper Eggs: Whisk egg yolks. Gradually add hot cream to yolks, whisking constantly. Return to saucepan.
3. Thicken: Cook over low heat, stirring until thickened (5-7 minutes). Do not boil.
4. Chill: Strain, stir in vanilla, peppermint, and food coloring (if using). Cool and refrigerate 4 hours.
5. Churn: Churn in an ice cream maker. Add chocolate chips in the last few minutes.
6. Freeze: Transfer to a container and freeze for 2 hours.

*Nutritional Information (Per Serving): Calories: 200  Protein: 3g  Carbs: 4g  Fats: 18g  Fiber: 1g*
*Cholesterol: 100mg  Sodium: 30mg  Potassium: 80mg*

---

# Strawberry Cheesecake Keto Ice Cream

**Prep Time: 15 minutes     Chill Time: 4 hours     Servings: 8**

## INGREDIENTS

- 2 cups heavy cream
- 1 cup unsweetened almond milk
- 1/2 cup erythritol
- 4 oz cream cheese, softened
- 1 tsp vanilla extract
- 4 large egg yolks
- 1 cup strawberries, chopped
- Optional: a few drops of red food coloring

## COOKING PROCESS

1. Heat Cream: Combine heavy cream, almond milk, and erythritol. Heat until it simmers, then remove from heat.
2. Temper Eggs: Whisk egg yolks. Gradually add hot cream to yolks, whisking constantly. Return to saucepan.
3. Thicken: Cook over low heat, stirring until thickened (5-7 minutes). Do not boil.
4. Blend with Cream Cheese: Strain mixture, then blend with cream cheese, vanilla, and food coloring (if using) until smooth. Cool and refrigerate 4 hours.
5. Churn: Churn in an ice cream maker. Add chopped strawberries in the last few minutes.
6. Freeze: Transfer to a container and freeze for 2 hours.

*Nutritional Information (Per Serving): Calories: 210  Protein: 3g  Carbs: 5g  Fats: 19g  Fiber: 1g*
*Cholesterol: 100mg  Sodium: 35mg  Potassium: 80mg*

# CHAPTER 7: DRINKS AND SMOOTHIES

# Bulletproof Coffee
**Prep Time: 5 minutes**    **Cook Time: 0 minutes**    **Servings: 1**

## INGREDIENTS
- 1 cup brewed coffee
- 1 tbsp unsalted butter
- 1 tbsp coconut oil or MCT oil
- Optional: 1 tsp vanilla extract or a pinch of cinnamon

## COOKING PROCESS
1. Brew Coffee: Brew your favorite coffee.
2. Blend Ingredients: In a blender, combine hot coffee, butter, and coconut oil (or MCT oil). Blend until frothy and well combined.
3. Serve: Pour into a mug and enjoy. Add vanilla extract or cinnamon if desired.

*Calories: 230 Protein: 0g Carbs: 0g Fats: 25g Fiber: 0g Cholesterol: 30mg Sodium: 5mg Potassium: 100mg*

# Keto Vanilla Chai Tea Latte
**Prep Time: 5 minutes**    **Cook Time: 5 minutes**    **Servings: 1**

## INGREDIENTS
- 1 chai tea bag
- 1 cup unsweetened almond milk
- 1 tbsp heavy cream
- 1 tbsp erythritol
- 1/2 tsp vanilla extract
- 1/4 tsp ground cinnamon
- Optional: whipped cream

## COOKING PROCESS
1. Brew Tea: Brew the chai tea bag in 1/2 cup hot water for 3-5 minutes.
2. Heat Milk: Warm almond milk and heavy cream in a saucepan over medium heat.
3. Combine: Mix brewed tea with warm milk. Add erythritol, vanilla, and cinnamon. Stir well.
4. Serve: Pour into a mug and top with whipped cream if desired.

*Calories: 120 Protein: 2g Carbs: 2g Fats: 11g Fiber: 0g Cholesterol: 35mg Sodium: 150mg Potassium: 100mg*

# Iced Matcha Coconut Latte
**Prep Time: 5 minutes**    **Cook Time: 0 minutes**    **Servings: 1**

## INGREDIENTS
- 1 tsp matcha powder
- 1/4 cup hot water
- 1 cup unsweetened coconut milk
- 1 tbsp erythritol or your preferred keto-friendly sweetener
- Ice cubes
- Optional: coconut flakes for garnish

## COOKING PROCESS
1. Prepare Matcha: Whisk matcha powder with hot water until smooth.
2. Mix: In a glass, combine coconut milk and erythritol. Stir well.
3. Combine: Pour the matcha mixture into the glass with coconut milk. Stir until well combined.
4. Serve: Add ice cubes and garnish with coconut flakes if desired.

*Calories: 70 Protein: 1g Carbs: 3g Fats: 6g Fiber: 1g Cholesterol: 0mg Sodium: 20mg Potassium: 50mg*

# Cinnamon Spiced Keto Coffee
**Prep Time: 5 minutes**    **Cook Time: 0 minutes**    **Servings: 1**

## INGREDIENTS
- 1 cup brewed coffee
- 1 tbsp unsalted butter
- 1 tbsp coconut oil or MCT oil
- 1/2 tsp ground cinnamon
- Optional: 1 tsp erythritol or your preferred keto-friendly sweetener

## COOKING PROCESS
1. Brew Coffee: Brew your favorite coffee.
2. Blend Ingredients: In a blender, combine hot coffee, butter, coconut oil (or MCT oil), and cinnamon. Blend until frothy and well combined.
3. Serve: Pour into a mug and enjoy. Add sweetener if desired.

*Calories: 220 Protein: 0g Carbs: 0g Fats: 25g Fiber: 0g Cholesterol: 30mg Sodium: 5mg Potassium: 100mg*

# Lemon and Mint Electrolyte Water

**Prep Time: 5 minutes    Cook Time: 0 minutes    Servings: 4**

## INGREDIENTS

- 1 lemon, sliced
- 1/4 cup fresh mint leaves
- 1/4 tsp salt
- 1/4 tsp baking soda
- 2 tbsp erythritol or your preferred keto-friendly sweetener
- 4 cups water
- Ice cubes

## COOKING PROCESS

1. Prepare Ingredients: In a large pitcher, combine sliced lemon, mint leaves, salt, baking soda, and erythritol.

2. Add Water: Pour in water and stir until well mixed.

3. Serve: Add ice cubes and stir again. Let sit for a few minutes to allow flavors to meld. Serve chilled.

*Calories: 0  Protein: 0g  Carbs: 0g  Fats: 0g  Fiber: 0g  Cholesterol: 0mg  Sodium: 150mg  Potassium: 10mg*

# Cucumber Lime Infused Water

**Prep Time: 5 minutes    Cook Time: 5 minutes    Servings: 1**

## INGREDIENTS

- 1 cucumber, sliced
- 1 lime, sliced
- 4 cups water
- Ice cubes
- Optional: fresh mint leaves for garnish

## COOKING PROCESS

1. Prepare Ingredients: In a large pitcher, combine cucumber slices and lime slices.

2. Add Water: Pour in water and stir.

3. Serve: Add ice cubes and let sit for a few minutes to infuse. Garnish with fresh mint leaves if desired. Serve chilled.

*Calories: 0  Protein: 0g  Carbs: 0g  Fats: 0g  Fiber: 0g  Cholesterol: 0mg  Sodium: 0mg  Potassium: 10mg*

# Berry Electrolyte Drink

**Prep Time: 5 minutes    Cook Time: 0 minutes    Servings: 4**

## INGREDIENTS

- 1/4 tsp baking soda
- 2 tbsp erythritol
- 1 cup mixed berries(strawberries, blueberries, raspberries)
- 1/4 tsp salt
- 4 cups water
- Ice cubes
- Optional: fresh mint leaves

## COOKING PROCESS

1. Blend Berries: Blend mixed berries with a small amount of water until smooth.

2. Mix Ingredients: In a pitcher, combine berry mixture, salt, baking soda, erythritol, and water. Stir well.

3. Serve: Add ice cubes. Garnish with mint leaves if desired. Serve chilled.

*Calories: 10  Protein: 0g  Carbs: 2g  Fats: 0g  Fiber: 1g  Cholesterol: 0mg  Sodium: 150mg  Potassium: 20mg*

# Citrus Ginger Detox Water

**Prep Time: 5 minutes    Cook Time: 0 minutes    Servings: 4**

## INGREDIENTS

- 1 lemon, sliced
- 1 lime, sliced
- 1 orange, sliced
- 1-inch piece ginger, sliced
- 4 cups water
- Ice cubes
- Optional: fresh mint leaves

## COOKING PROCESS

1. Mix Ingredients: Combine lemon, lime, orange, and ginger slices in a pitcher. Add water and stir.

2. Serve: Add ice. Let sit to infuse. Garnish with mint if desired. Serve chilled.

*Calories: 5  Protein: 0g  Carbs: 1g  Fats: 0g  Fiber: 0g  Cholesterol: 0mg  Sodium: 0mg  Potassium: 20mg*

# Spinach Avocado Keto Smoothie
## Prep Time: 5 minutes    Cook Time: 0 minutes    Servings: 2

**INGREDIENTS**

- 1 avocado, peeled and pitted
- 1 cup fresh spinach leaves
- 1 cup unsweetened almond milk
- 1/2 cup water
- 1 tbsp chia seeds
- Ice cubes
- 1 tbsp erythritol or your preferred keto-friendly sweetener
- 1 tsp vanilla extract

**COOKING PROCESS**

1. Blend Ingredients: Combine avocado, spinach, almond milk, water, chia seeds, erythritol, vanilla extract, and ice cubes in a blender. Blend until smooth.
2. Serve: Pour into glasses and serve immediately.

*Calories: 180  Protein: 3g  Carbs: 8g  Fats: 15g  Fiber: 6g  Cholesterol: 0mg  Sodium: 40mg  Potassium: 500mg*

# Kale and Coconut Green Smoothie
## Prep Time: 5 minutes    Cook Time: 5 minutes    Servings: 2

**INGREDIENTS**

- 1 cup kale leaves
- 1/2 avocado
- 1 cup unsweetened coconut milk
- 1/2 cup water
- 1 tbsp chia seeds
- 1 tbsp erythritol
- 1 tsp vanilla extract
- Ice cubes

**COOKING PROCESS**

1. Blend Ingredients: Combine kale, avocado, coconut milk, water, chia seeds, erythritol, vanilla extract, and ice cubes in a blender. Blend until smooth.
2. Serve: Pour into glasses and serve immediately.

*Calories: 160  Protein: 3g  Carbs: 7g  Fats: 14g  Fiber: 5g  Cholesterol: 0mg  Sodium: 30mg  Potassium: 450mg*

# Cucumber Mint Green Smoothie
## Prep Time: 5 minutes    Cook Time: 0 minutes    Servings: 2

**INGREDIENTS**

- 1 cucumber, chopped
- 1 cup spinach
- 1/4 cup mint leaves
- 1/2 avocado
- 1 cup unsweetened almond milk
- 1 tbsp chia seeds
- 1 tbsp erythritol
- Ice cubes

**COOKING PROCESS**

1. Blend: Combine cucumber, spinach, mint, avocado, almond milk, chia seeds, erythritol, and ice cubes in a blender. Blend until smooth.
2. Serve: Pour into glasses and serve.

*Calories: 120  Protein: 2g  Carbs: 6g  Fats: 10g  Fiber: 4g  Cholesterol: 0mg  Sodium: 30mg  Potassium: 350mg*

# Green Detox Smoothie with Chia Seeds
## Prep Time: 5 minutes    Cook Time: 0 minutes    Servings: 2

**INGREDIENTS**

- 1 cup spinach
- 1/2 cucumber, chopped
- 1/2 green apple, chopped
- 1/2 avocado
- 1 cup unsweetened almond milk
- 1 tbsp chia seeds
- 1 tbsp lemon juice
- Ice cubes

**COOKING PROCESS**

1. Blend: Combine all ingredients in a blender. Blend until smooth.
2. Serve: Pour into glasses and serve.

*Calories: 150  Protein: 3g  Carbs: 10g  Fats: 10g  Fiber: 6g  Cholesterol: 0mg  Sodium: 40mg  Potassium: 400mg*

# Chocolate Almond Butter Protein Smoothie

**Prep Time: 5 minutes**    **Cook Time: 0 minutes**    **Servings: 2**

## INGREDIENTS

- 1 cup unsweetened almond milk
- 2 tbsp almond butter
- 1 scoop chocolate protein powder (keto-friendly)
- 1 tbsp unsweetened cocoa powder
- 1/2 avocado
- 1 tbsp chia seeds
- Ice cubes

## COOKING PROCESS

1. Blend: Combine all ingredients in a blender. Blend until smooth.
2. Serve: Pour into glasses and serve.

*Calories: 250  Protein: 15g  Carbs: 7g  Fats: 20g  Fiber: 5g  Cholesterol: 0mg  Sodium: 150mg  Potassium: 400mg*

---

# Vanilla Coconut Protein Shake

**Prep Time: 5 minutes**    **Cook Time: 0 minutes**    **Servings: 1**

## INGREDIENTS

- 1 cup unsweetened coconut milk
- 1 scoop vanilla protein powder (keto-friendly)
- 1/2 cup unsweetened shredded coconut
- 1 tbsp chia seeds
- 1 tsp vanilla extract
- Ice cubes

## COOKING PROCESS

1. Blend: Combine all ingredients in a blender. Blend until smooth.
2. Serve: Pour into glasses and serve.

*Calories: 200  Protein: 15g  Carbs: 5g  Fats: 15g  Fiber: 4g  Cholesterol: 0mg  Sodium: 100mg  Potassium: 200mg*

---

# Berry Keto Protein Smoothie

**Prep Time: 5 minutes**    **Cook Time: 0 minutes**    **Servings: 2**

## INGREDIENTS

- 1 cup unsweetened almond milk
- 1/2 cup mixed berries (strawberries, blueberries, raspberries)
- 1 scoop vanilla protein powder (keto-friendly)
- 1 tbsp chia seeds
- 1 tbsp erythritol or your preferred keto-friendly sweetener
- Ice cubes

## COOKING PROCESS

1. Blend: Combine all ingredients in a blender. Blend until smooth.
2. Serve: Pour into glasses and serve.

*Calories: 150  Protein: 15g  Carbs: 7g  Fats: 8g  Fiber: 4g  Cholesterol: 0mg  Sodium: 100mg  Potassium: 200mg*

---

# Peanut Butter and Banana Protein Smoothie

**Prep Time: 5 minutes**    **Cook Time: 0 minutes**    **Servings: 2**

## INGREDIENTS

- 1 cup unsweetened almond milk
- 1 scoop vanilla protein powder (keto-friendly)
- 2 tbsp peanut butter (no sugar added)
- 1 small banana
- 1 tbsp chia seeds
- Ice cubes

## COOKING PROCESS

1. Blend: Combine all ingredients in a blender. Blend until smooth.
2. Serve: Pour into glasses and serve.

*Calories: 220  Protein: 0g  Carbs: 0g  Fats: 25g  Fiber: 0g  Cholesterol: 30mg  Sodium: 5mg  Potassium: 100mg*

# CHAPTER 8: 30-DAY MEAL PLAN

# MEAL PLANNER

## WEEK 1

| | BREAKFAST | LUNCH | DINNER | SNACKS |
|---|---|---|---|---|
| MON | Cheesy Spinach and Mushroom Keto Omelette | Grilled Chicken Caesar Keto Salad | Garlic Butter Chicken Thighs with Asparagus | Spicy Roasted Almonds and Pumpkin Seeds |
| TUE | Berry Avocado Delight Smoothie | Creamy Broccoli Cheddar Keto Soup | Slow-Cooker Chicken Alfredo | Italian Antipasto Platter with Mozzarella and Prosciutto |
| WED | Fluffy Almond Flour Keto Pancakes | Keto Beef Burrito Bowl | Lemon Garlic Butter Salmon | Creamy Avocado and Spinach Dip |
| THU | Sausage and Cheese Keto Breakfast Casserole | Asian Beef Keto Lettuce Wraps | Spinach and Feta Stuffed Portobello Mushrooms | Zucchini Parmesan Crisps |
| FRI | Crispy Almond Flour Keto Waffles | Keto Chicken and Mushroom Soup | Creamy Seafood Chowder | Cinnamon Pecan and Walnut Trail Mix |
| SAT | Bacon-Wrapped Avocado Bites | Cilantro Lime Cauliflower Rice | Cauliflower Mac and Cheese | Cheddar and Salami Snack Platter |
| SUN | Creamy Coconut Matcha Smoothie | Grilled Salmon and Avocado Keto Bowl | Broccoli Cheddar Soup | Smoky Bacon and Cheddar Cheese Spread |

# MEAL PLANNER

WEEK 2

| | BREAKFAST | LUNCH | DINNER | SNACKS |
|---|---|---|---|---|
| MON | Bacon and Avocado Keto Egg Muffins | Rich and Creamy Tomato Basil Keto Soup | Beef and Broccoli Stir-Fry | Mini Bacon-Wrapped Meatballs |
| TUE | Coconut Flour Blueberry Keto Pancakes | Turkey and Cheese Keto Lettuce Wraps | Instant Pot Beef Stew | Savory Herb Cashew and Sunflower Seed Mix |
| WED | Spinach, Bacon, and Feta Keto Breakfast Bake | Keto Chicken Pesto Zoodle Bowl | Pork Chops with Creamy Mushroom Sauce | Greek Mezze Platter with Feta and Olives |
| THU | Cinnamon Vanilla Keto Waffles | Keto Clam Chowder | Shrimp Scampi with Zoodles | Garlic and Herb Cream Cheese Dip |
| FRI | Keto Avocado Bacon Egg Salad | Cauliflower Rice Risotto with Mushrooms | Zucchini Noodles with Pesto | Cheesy Cauliflower Tots |
| SAT | Green Detox Keto Smoothie | Pork and Cauliflower Rice Keto Bowl | Spicy Shrimp and Sausage Stew | Coconut Flaxseed and Chia Seed Crunch |
| SUN | Keto Eggs Benedict with Hollandaise Sauce | Spinach and Feta Keto Greek Salad | Eggplant Parmesan | Swiss and Roast Beef Roll-Ups |

# MEAL PLANNER

## WEEK 3

| | BREAKFAST | LUNCH | DINNER | SNACKS |
|---|---|---|---|---|
| MON | Cream Cheese Keto Pancakes | Keto Bacon and Cauliflower Chowder | Roasted Brussels Sprouts with Bacon | Spicy Jalapeno and Artichoke Dip |
| TUE | Mexican Chorizo and Egg Keto Breakfast Casserole | Chicken Avocado Keto Lettuce Wraps | Herb-Crusted Lamb Chops | Stuffed Mushroom Caps with Sausage and Cream Cheese |
| WED | Cheddar Chive Savory Keto Waffles | Steak and Avocado Protein Bowl | Slow-Cooker Pulled Pork | Rosemary Garlic Almonds and Pecans |
| THU | Creamy Avocado and Bacon Zoodles | Tuna and Egg Keto Salad with Lemon Dressing | Keto BBQ Pork Ribs with a side of Coleslaw | Pepper Jack and Turkey Platter |
| FRI | Vanilla Almond Protein Smoothie | Creamy Asparagus Soup | Baked Cod with Herb Butter | Sun-Dried Tomato and Olive Tapenade |
| SAT | Creamy Garlic Parmesan Keto Scrambled Eggs | Turkey and Spinach Power Bowl | Cauliflower Crust Margherita Pizza | Roasted Red Pepper and Walnut Dip |
| SUN | Lemon Ricotta Keto Pancakes | Tuna Poke Keto Bowl | Fish and Tomato Stew | Bacon and Cheddar Stuffed Jalapenos |

# MEAL PLANNER

WEEK 4

| | BREAKFAST | LUNCH | DINNER | SNACKS |
|---|---|---|---|---|
| MON | Chocolate Hazelnut Keto Waffles | Herbed Keto Flatbread | Cauliflower Fried Rice | Maple Vanilla Macadamia and Hemp Seed Mix |
| TUE | Mushroom and Swiss Keto Breakfast Casserole | Keto Beef Bulgogi Bowl | Beef and Vegetable Kebabs | Brie and Smoked Salmon Platter |
| WED | Keto BLT Avocado Bowls | Zucchini and Parmesan Soup | Instant Pot Lamb Curry | Smoky Paprika Walnuts and Pumpkin Seeds |
| THU | Scrambled Eggs with Spinach and Avocado | Fluffy Coconut Flour Keto Biscuits | Creamy Garlic Mushroom and Spinach Skillet | Creamy Blue Cheese Dip |
| FRI | Blueberry Coconut Keto Waffles | Spicy Shrimp Keto Lettuce Wraps | Grilled Tuna Steaks with Avocado Salsa | Garlic Butter Shrimp Skewers |
| SAT | Bacon and Broccoli Breakfast Bake | Cilantro Lime Cauliflower Rice | Spaghetti Squash Alfredo with Roasted Vegetables | Lemon Zest Almond and Flaxseed Blend |
| SUN | Avocado Bacon Deviled Eggs | Rich and Creamy Tomato Basil Keto Soup | Stuffed Bell Peppers with Quinoa and Cheese | Keto Pimento Cheese Spread |

# MEAL PLANNER

WEEK 5

| | BREAKFAST | LUNCH | DINNER | SNACKS |
|---|---|---|---|---|
| MON | Omelette with Tomatoes, Basil, and Mozzarella | Cauliflower and Cheese Soup | Slow-Cooker Chicken Alfredo | Keto Deviled Eggs |
| TUE | Pumpkin Spice Keto Waffles | Almond Flour Keto Bread Loaf | Stuffed Bell Peppers with Ground Turkey | Keto Chicken Tenders |
| WED | | | | |
| THU | | | | |
| FRI | | | | |
| SAT | | | | |
| SUN | | | | |

# CHAPTER 9: TIPS AND TRICKS FOR SUCCESS

# Staying on Track
## Dealing with keto flu

Starting a ketogenic diet can lead to a set of temporary, flu-like symptoms known as "keto flu." Understanding and managing these symptoms can help you transition to ketosis more comfortably.

**What is Keto Flu?**

Keto flu occurs when your body adapts to burning fat for fuel instead of carbohydrates. Common symptoms include:

- Headache
- Dizziness
- Irritability
- Difficulty sleeping
- Fatigue
- Nausea
- Muscle cramps
- Brain fog

**Why Does Keto Flu Happen?**

1. Glycogen Depletion: Reduced carbs lead to depleted glycogen stores and temporary fatigue.
2. Electrolyte Imbalance: Loss of glycogen and water causes increased urination and electrolyte loss.
3. Adaptation to Ketosis: Your body needs time to adjust to burning fat for fuel.

**How to Manage Keto Flu**

1. **Stay Hydrated:**
   - Drink plenty of water.
   - Add a pinch of salt or drink electrolyte-rich beverages.
2. **Increase Electrolyte Intake:**
   - Eat potassium-rich foods (avocados, spinach, nuts).
   - Incorporate magnesium-rich foods (leafy greens, seeds).
   - Consider electrolyte supplements if needed.
3. **Eat Enough Fat:**
   - Consume healthy fats like avocados, olive oil, and fatty meats.
4. **Gradually Reduce Carbs:**
   - Slowly decrease carbohydrate intake over a week or two.
5. **Get Plenty of Rest:**
   - Ensure adequate sleep and rest.
   - Practice good sleep hygiene.
6. **Stay Active:**
   - Engage in light to moderate exercise like walking or yoga.
   - Avoid intense workouts initially.
7. **Listen to Your Body:**
   - Pay attention to how you feel and adjust as needed.
   - Consult a healthcare professional if symptoms persist or worsen.

# Tips for eating out

1. **Do Your Research**. Before venturing out peruse the restaurants menu. Seek out keto selections or dishes that can be easily tweaked to align with your requirements. Many restaurants nowadays offer options tailored for keto eaters.

2. **Personalize Your Order**. Feel free to request alterations. Most restaurants are open to accommodating needs. Here are some common tweaks you can ask for:
- Substitute carbs with veggies: Exchange bread, pasta, or rice for vegetables or a side salad.
- Skip the starch: Request your sans potatoes, fries, or other starchy accompaniments.
- Opt for fats: Ask for avocado, olive oil, or butter to amp up your fat consumption.

3. **Emphasize Protein and Vegetables**. Opt, for dishes that highlight protein and non starchy veggies. Grilled meats, fish and salads are typically choices. Steer clear of fried items as they tend to harbor concealed carbs.

4. **Be mindful when it comes to sauces and dressings**. Many of them have added sugars and carbs. It's an idea to request them on the side and use them in moderation. Opt for olive oil, vinegar, or lemon juice as dressings whenever you can.

5. **Skip the Bread Basket**. Politely pass on the bread basket. Kindly ask your server not to bring it to your table. By doing this you can avoid the temptation. Focus better on your keto objectives.

6. **Drink Smart**. Make beverage choices by sticking with water, iced tea or sparkling water. If you decide to have alcohol go for options, like dry wine, spirits or light beer while avoiding sugary mixers.

7. **Watch Out for Hidden Carbs**. Be cautious of carbs that could sneak into your meal through ingredients like croutons, tortilla strips or sweetened sauces. When in doubt about a dishs contents don't hesitate to inquire about them.

8. **Plan Your Portions**. Keep an eye on portion sizes at restaurants since they tend to be generous. Consider sharing a meal or taking half of it home to prevent overeating. This strategy not helps you stay true, to your goals but also ensures you have a keto meal for later.

9. **Look for Keto-Friendly Restaurants**. Seek out restaurants that offer keto options specifically tailored for carb and keto diets.
Look for these places for choices and a menu that suits your requirements.

10. **Share Your Preferences**. Feel free to let your server know about your needs. They can offer suggestions. Ensure that your meal meets your keto requirements.

Example of a Keto-Friendly Restaurant Meal
- Appetizer: Avocado and shrimp cocktail (without the cocktail sauce)
- Main Course: Grilled salmon with spinach on the side, along with a garden salad dressed with olive oil and vinegar
- Dessert: Cheese platter (without the crackers) or fresh berries topped with whipped cream

# Adjusting your macros as you progress

**Why Adjust Your Macros?**

1. Weight Loss Plateaus: Your caloric needs decrease as you lose weight.
2. Increased Activity: More activity may require more protein and fat.
3. Changing Goals: Building muscle or improving performance may need macro tweaks.

**How to Adjust Your Macros**

1. Recalculate Caloric Needs:
   - Use an online calculator based on your current weight and activity level.
2. Adjust Protein Intake:
   - Weight Loss: Keep protein moderate to preserve muscle.
   - Muscle Gain: Increase protein slightly.
3. Modify Fat Intake:
   - Weight Loss: Reduce fat to create a caloric deficit.
   - Increased Activity: Increase fat for more energy.
4. Monitor Carbs:
   - Stay under 20-50 grams of net carbs per day.
5. Track Progress:
   - Use a food diary or app to monitor your macros and body's response.

**Practical Tips**

1. Listen to Your Body:
   - Adjust if you feel tired or hungry.
2. Stay Flexible:
   - Be ready to tweak your macros as needed.
3. Consult a Professional:
   - Get help from a nutritionist or dietitian if unsure.

**Sample Adjustments**

1. Weight Loss Plateau:
   - Original: 75% fat, 20% protein, 5% carbs
   - Adjusted: 70% fat, 25% protein, 5% carbs
2. Increased Activity:
   - Original: 70% fat, 25% protein, 5% carbs
   - Adjusted: 75% fat, 20% protein, 5% carbs

**Monitoring Progress**

1. Weekly Weigh-Ins:
   - Track your weight to see trends.
2. Body Measurements:
   - Measure key areas to assess changes.
3. Energy Levels:
   - Note how you feel throughout the day.
4. Ketone Levels:
   - Use ketone test strips to ensure ketosis.

# Alphabetical Recipe Index

## Breakfast

## Lunch

## Dinner

# Alphabetical Recipe Index

Made in the USA
Las Vegas, NV
19 September 2024